THE COMPLETE AQUARIUM PROBLEM SOLVER

A Total Trouble-Shooting Guide for Freshwater and Marine Aquariums

KEVIN W. BOYD

Cover: Percula Clownfish
Cover Design: Chuck Barrett

Tetra⬤Press

Tetra Sales U.S.A.
3001 Commerce Street
Blacksburg, VA 24060

The Complete Aquarium Problem Solver

A Total Trouble-Shooting Guide for Freshwater and Marine Aquariums

Kevin W. Boyd

Published by:

BOYLEN, INC.
P.O. BOX 65
BATAVIA, IL 60510 U.S.A.

Distributed by:

Tetra◉Press

TETRA SALES U.S.A.
3001 COMMERCE STREET
BLACKSBURG, VA 24060

Library of Congress Cataloging in Publication Data
Boyd, Kevin W.
The Complete Aquarium Problem Solver: A Total Trouble-Shooting Guide for Freshwater and Marine Aquariums / by Kevin W. Boyd.

Bibliography
1. Aquariums
2. Aquarium Fishes
CIP 90-093274
ISBN 1-56465-142-8: Hardcover
Printed in the United States of America

Sixth Printing

Tetra Press Item #16099

How To Use This Book...

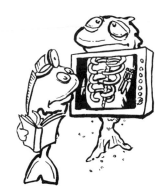

Trouble-shooting aquarium problems and diagnosing fish diseases can be a difficult and time consuming task. To help ease these problems, this book has been divided into three sections, each covering a specific component of the aquarium hobby - **General Problems, Equipment Problems** and **Fish Diseases**. You should use the book in the following manner.

1) Start with the Flow Charts - No matter what the aquarium problem is, always begin with the flow charts that are located in the middle of the book. These nine, fold out, trouble-shooting flow charts will guide you to the most likely cause of the aquarium problem, equipment problem or fish disease. Be sure to read and carefully follow the **FLOW CHART INSTRUCTIONS** before you begin.

2) Identify the Correct File - After using the flow charts to make a diagnosis, a particular "file" will be identified for you to read. These files explain what the aquarium problem is, what the symptoms are and how to solve the problem.

3) Locate the File - The file that is identified in the flow charts as your particular aquarium problem will be located in one of the three sections of the book; **General Problems, Equipment Problems** or **Fish Diseases**. Turn to the **File Contents** in the front of the book. Each section is represented by a file cabinet. The files are in alphabetical order in the file cabinet so you can easily find the page number of the identified file. Now turn to the page number given and read how to solve the problem. You need only to read the file identified as your aquarium problem.

Fish Disease Photos
Included in the Fish Disease section are color photos of some of the more common fish diseases. Use the flow charts first to make the proper diagnosis and then refer to the photos for a secondary confirmation only.

Appendix
For your convenience, an **Index** as well as useful **Conversion Tables, Formulas, Charts** and **Graphs** are provided in the back of the book.

Please Notice
The full potential of this book is met when it is used with the book *The Complete Aquarium Logbook*, available at your aquarium dealer from **Tetra Press**. Use the problem solving book to diagnose fish and aquatic animal diseases, or to trouble-shoot water and equipment problems. Then use the Logbook to record all problems discovered, therapy given or repairs made.

Dedication

I wish to dedicate this book to my loving wife, Judy, for her patience and understanding of my fish hobby (such as overlooking spilled saltwater on the floor), and for her support throughout the writing of this book; and to my parents, who have always encouraged my dreams.

Acknowledgements

This book could not have been written without the knowledge, creativity and support of several key individuals. Sincere thanks to Roger Klocek, the Curator of Fishes at the John G. Shedd Aquarium in Chicago, Illinois, who offered valuable information that can only come from years of experience in fish parasitology. I am grateful to the individual pet shop owners whom I interviewed to confirm many of the problems and solutions offered in this book. The owners knew and communicated their customer's problems well.

Thanks also to Joanne Mullin for her excellent editing and creative writing ideas; my wife for all her assistance with the manuscript; Steve Arnold for the layout of the flow charts; Lynn Burnoski for her equipment and morphology illustrations; and to fellow aquarist Al Ochsner for his appropriately amusing cartoons. Special thanks to Chuck Barrett for the cover design, fish disease illustrations and overall layout.

About the Author

Kevin W. Boyd has been an avid saltwater aquarist for many years and has dedicated his hobby to the study of marine and freshwater aquarium problems and solutions. Kevin is also the author of *The Complete Aquarium Logbook*. He holds two Master's degrees and is a former professional musician. Kevin lives and works in the Chicago suburbs.

If you would like information on obtaining a copy of one of the cartoons used in this book, write to Ostudio, PO Box 421, Geneva, IL 60134

A FEW THOUGHTS BEFORE YOU BEGIN...

Establish Your Aquarium
The Complete Aquarium Problem Solver is dedicated solely to solving the problems of fish hobbyists. This manual was written with the assumption that you already have an established aquarium. "Established" means that your aquarium has been properly set up, has gone through its natural biological filter cycle, and has been relatively successful for at least six weeks. If you are new to the hobby, you should also purchase a book on setting up an aquarium.

The Key to Success is Early Recognition of Problems
The most important factor in successful treatment of fish disease or aquarium problems is early recognition of the problem. The only way to accomplish this is by daily observation of your aquarium. Become familiar with the normal size, shape and coloration; as well as the regular swimming, feeding and sleeping habits of each fish, plant or animal. If any of these factors suddenly change, it could be an early indication of problems or disease.

Don't Overreact
Remember, fish do act differently on occasion, even when there is no problem. If you notice a problem, don't immediately overreact. Instead, observe the entire aquarium with discretion.

Check Environmental Conditions First
Once you have noticed a change with a fish, animal or plant, use the **Water and Equipment Problems Flow Charts** to be sure that the tank's environmental conditions are ideal. If you don't find a problem, observe the fish closely, noting any abnormal symptoms. If the condition continues or worsens after one day, or, if that fish or other fish, begin to show other abnormal symptoms, consider the problem serious enough to diagnose it by using the **Fish Problems Flow Charts**.

Act Fast
Once you determine that the fish is diseased, immediate action is needed in order to control the disease. Waiting even three days for treatment can allow some diseases enough time to reproduce by as much as one thousand times. In most cases, when a fish dies from disease, it is because the aquarist has waited too long before taking action.

Read Only the "File" You Need
This book is not intended to be read from cover to cover. The objective is to provide quick, accurate information. The book is divided into several "files" on individual subjects. Once you have diagnosed the problem, you need only read the file for that subject.

Diagnoses
A diagnosis given in the flow charts does not always mean that your fish has that particular disease. The diagnosis means that, based on the symptoms of your fish, it should be treated according to the particular disease mentioned.

Medications and Treatment
In many of the treatment sections for a problem or disease, there are specific directions provided for the proper conditions in which the disease should be treated. If at any time the pharmaceutical manufacturer's directions conflict with this manual's recommendations, follow the manufacturer's directions. The only exception is when these directions suggest that the drug be added directly to the main tank. Drugs should not be added to the main tank. The reasons for this are stated in the **HOSPITAL TANK** section.

Specific brand medications are not recommended because new drugs are being introduced every few months. Once you have reached a diagnosis from the flow charts, ask your fish dealer which medication has been most successful in treating the particular disease. Compare the drugs listed on the medication label with what is listed in this manual's treatment section for the disease. If they match, that medication is your best choice. Avoid the "cure all" drugs that claim to cure many types of disease. Experience has shown them to be the least effective. Instead, purchase a medication that is manufactured specifically for the diagnosed disease.

Prevention is Always Better than a Cure

Don't use this manual as a crutch for your aquarium problems. Perform daily checks of all fish and equipment as summarized in **WATER CHEMISTRY** and ensure proper nutrition described in **FEEDING**. If these environmental conditions are ideal, you will eliminate most of your potential aquarium problems.

Learn From Mistakes

Remember also, that sometimes, despite your best efforts, your fish or animal will die. If you have done your best, consider it part of the hobby. Note any mistakes, learn as much as you can from the experience, and try not to repeat the same mistakes in the future.

Stay Informed

A well informed aquarist has the best possible chance of keeping a successful aquarium. Expand your personal library to include other books on fish diseases. Subscribe to magazines about the fish hobby and check for books on fish at the library. If you live near a large city you may be fortunate enough to have a fish veterinarian or marine biologist in the area on whom you can call for advice. Remember, zoos and especially public aquariums have qualified individuals who can provide valuable information about your hobby and help solve your aquarium problems.

Reader Please Note

This manual is intended as a guide to help diagnose and solve general aquarium problems. The information used in this book is based upon the experience of professionals in the field of aquariums and fish parasitology. The information is generalized to render the best possible diagnosis based solely on observation by the hobbyist. Please note that aquarium problems and especially fish diseases are complex and in some cases cannot be definitively diagnosed from observation alone. Even when properly used, this manual is not the equivalent of specialized laboratory tests or a trained fish veterinarian. Therefore, BoyLen Inc. and the author are not responsible for misdiagnoses, the cost of equipment repair or replacement, treatment, or the death of your fish, animal, or plant even when properly treated under the guidelines of this manual.

Kevin W. Boyd

File Contents

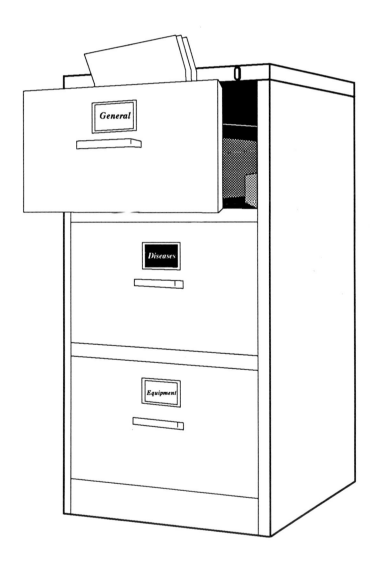

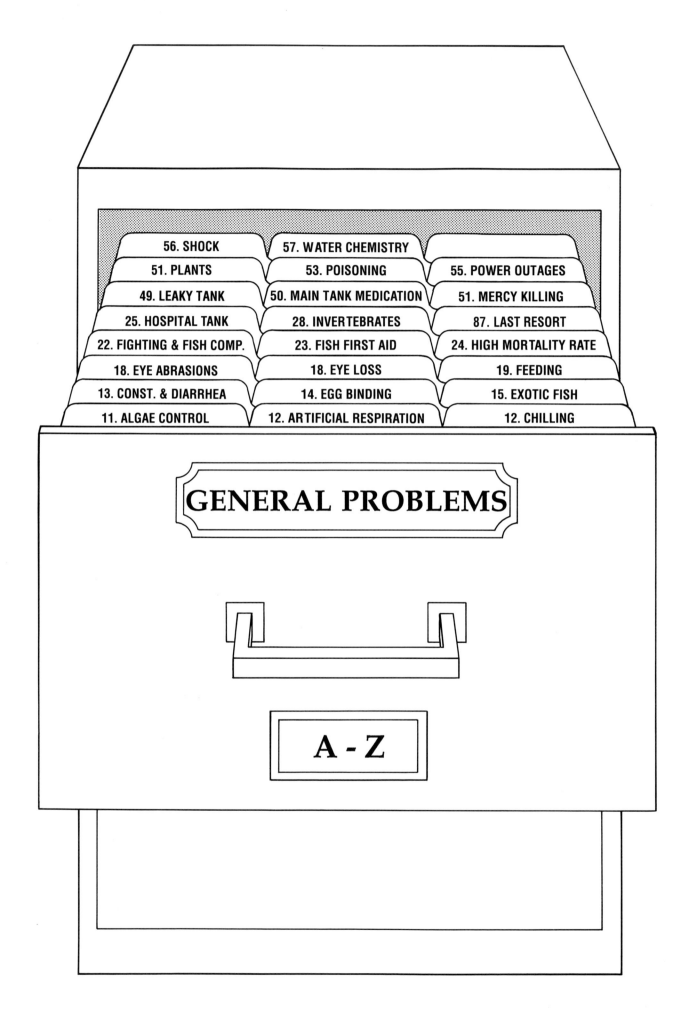

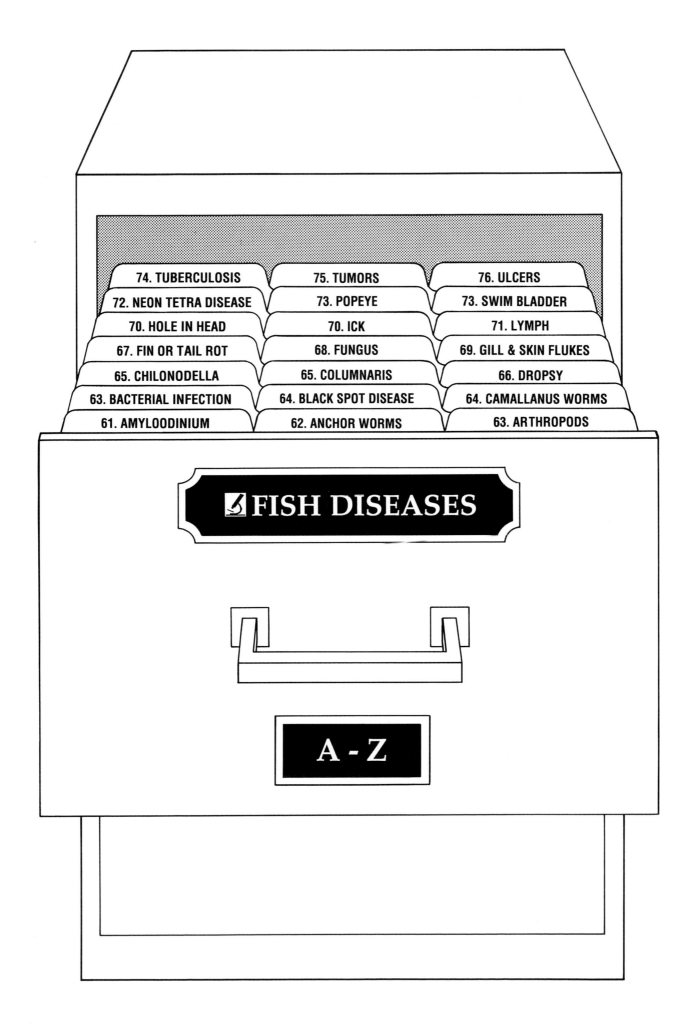

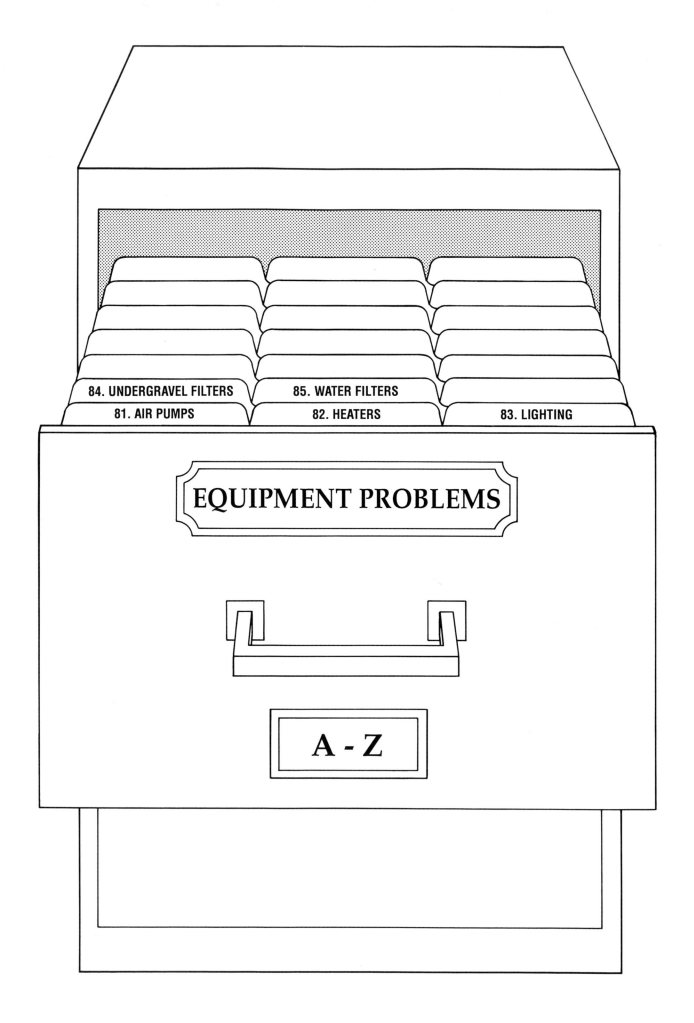

GENERAL PROBLEMS

ALGAE CONTROL

If you have to scrape green algae from the sides of the tank every few weeks, congratulations, your tank has healthy water conditions! Algae is an essential part of the aquarium's natural biological filter. In marine tanks, algae acts as a supplemental filter by using carbon dioxide which in turn keeps the pH level up and the nitrates down. No aquarium should be without some green algae. However, too much algae can cause respiratory problems and may eventually become toxic to your fish. Therefore, algae control is a necessary part of proper aquarium maintenance.

Algae is a form of plant life that needs proper water conditions and sufficient light in order to grow. So, if there is no algae, or if the algae is brown instead of green, your tank has either poor water quality or insufficient light (see **WATER CHEMISTRY**).

Algae Control: Healthy green algae should be allowed to grow on rocks and coral in the tank. However, you may want to remove the algae from some decorative rocks and coral. This is best accomplished by removing these pieces, and placing them in a sink. Pour boiling water over the rocks and coral, then allow a few minutes of cooling before placing them back in the tank. Be careful when pouring boiling water on fragile coral because it can cause the coral to crack. In a few days the algae will die and the decorative pieces will be restored to their original color.

Algae should be scraped from the sides of the tank glass with a proper algae scraper sponge. Never use metal as a scraper because it may scratch the glass, and, no metals should ever be placed in the tank.

Algae medications should be avoided unless the algae has become uncontrollable. A better solution would be to stock an algae-eating herbivore fish (plant eater, see **FEEDING**) and enjoy watching it eat the algae as it constantly picks over the rocks. Snails can also be used for algae cleaning purposes. However, snails can quickly overrun the tank if not kept under control (see **INVERTEBRATES**).

If the tank water has a greenish tint, it is probably from excessive algal growth, and can cause respiratory problems in fish. In this case, scrape as much of the algae as possible and perform an immediate 50 percent water change. If little improvement is noticed after two days, perform an additional 25 percent water change.

Allow carbon filters to run, and increase aeration for one day after the water change. The secret to proper algal growth is to provide proper water quality and lighting, stock at least one herbivore, and perform a weekly algae scraping of the tank glass to keep the algae growth under control.

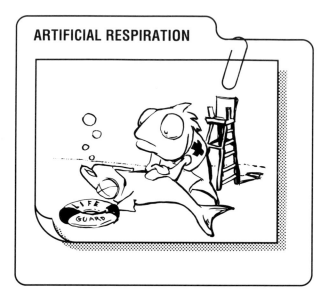

ARTIFICIAL RESPIRATION

Some fish develop physical problems that may severely, but temporarily, hinder their breathing. Artificial respiration for fish simply consists of helping the fish breath by artificially running water over the fish's gills. Severely irregular breathing exhibited by a fish (that is not the result of disease) can be caused by such problems as poisoning, an adverse reaction to medication, very poor water conditions such as lack of aeration, the fish receiving a hard blow from a tankmate, being frightened or in shock, or even jumping out of the tank. If you notice sudden, irregular or severe breathing problems with your fish, artificial respiration is quickly needed, or death may occur.

Symptoms: The fish appears to hyperventilate, or exhibits unusually fast, slow or irregular breathing patterns. The fish may not be able to breath, may also be listless or lying on the tank bottom. The breathing problem occurred suddenly and there are no symptoms of disease.

Treatment: Net the affected fish and leave the net in the water near the surface. Very slowly, move the net back and forth with long sweeps of the arm. This causes the water to flow over the fish's gills enabling it to artificially breath. The treatment should continue for a few minutes, until the fish begins to recover. If the fish does not respond to this treatment, the problem is severe, and the fish may not recover.

Note: If the fish has been poisoned, artificial respiration must be performed in freshly prepared water (refer to **POISONING**). If the fish has been wounded, once it is breathing normally, refer then to **FISH FIRST AID** for proper treatment.

CHILLING

Chilling refers to a reaction that fish have after being subjected to cool or cold water. In many cases, the symptoms are the early signs of other problems or diseases. If the tank has been exposed to cool drafts, the room has been cold, the heater is not working properly or cold water has been poured into the tank during a water change, your fish may suffer from chilling.

To avoid chilling, ensure proper water conditions and match the temperature of the replacement water to the tank water temperature when making water changes. Refer to **WATER CHEMISTRY**.

Symptoms: The fish exhibits equilibrium problems, such as rocking, wobbling, or sluggish behavior. The fish remains stationary while fanning its pectoral fins to maintain balance. The fish's eyes may also become cloudy or hazy.

Treatment: If the tank is too cold, adjust the heater to raise the water temperature slowly, by one degree every five hours, until it reaches normal temperature (77 degrees is ideal). If your heater is not functioning properly, go to the **Equipment Problems Flow Chart** to determine the cause. If the water temperature is normal, but the water was recently "chilled," wait two to four days to determine whether the fish returns to normal.

If the fish's symptoms remain after five days, or, if at any time, they worsen, the problem is not chilling, but disease. Use the **Fish Problems Flow Charts** to determine the disease. If no other symptoms are found, treat the fish according to **ICK** and observe the fish closely for signs of other disease.

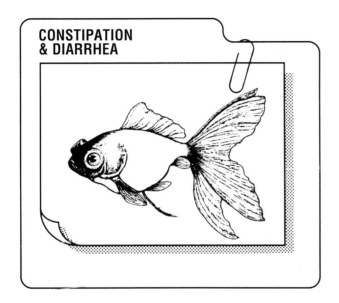

CONSTIPATION
& DIARRHEA

If a fish has been fed an improper diet or is subjected to poor water conditions, it may develop constipation or diarrhea. Diarrhea can also be caused from eating a steady diet of frozen foods. Make sure that you thaw frozen foods in a glass of tank water before you place them in the tank.

Constipation Symptoms: A string of feces trails behind the fish, the abdomen swells, the fish has little interest in food, and the fish is sluggish or resting on the bottom. No symptoms of disease are present.

Constipation Treatment: Do not feed the fish for two days. Separate it from its tankmates during feeding times with a glass partition, if possible. After the fast, feed the fish herbivore plant and vegetable foods (see **FEEDING**) such as romaine lettuce, algae, green peas or guinea pig food pellets, for the next two days. After the treatment period, remember to feed a proper and varied diet. Refer to **FEEDING** to determine the correct foods for your fish.

If the varied diet does not help, or if the constipation is severe and is causing much distress to the fish, it can be treated with cod liver oil. Net the fish and place it on a clean, wet towel. Place two drops of cod liver oil directly in the mouth of the fish and place it back in the main tank. Don't leave the fish out of the water for more than one minute. The fish should not be fed for two days after treatment.

Diarrhea Symptoms: The fish has extremely loose feces, is disinterested in food, and may have a swollen body. No symptoms of disease are present.

Diarrhea Treatment: Don't let the affected fish eat for two days. Separate it from its tankmates during feeding times with a glass partition, if possible. After the fast, feed flakes and carnivore foods (see **FEEDING**) for three days. Refer to **FEEDING** to determine the proper food for your fish. Remember to vary the fish's diet.

Note: Internal diseases can also give the same symptoms as constipation or diarrhea. If the fish does not respond to the preceding treatments, or if its condition worsens, assume the problem is caused by disease and treat as described below.

Disease Treatment: For the symptoms of constipation, treat the fish with a wide spectrum antibiotic according to **BACTERIAL INFECTION**. For symptoms of diarrhea, treat for Hexamita according to **HOLE IN HEAD**. In addition, for either problem, also feed the fish with medicated fish food, according to **CAMALLANUS WORMS**. For either disease, treatment should be given in a separate hospital tank. See **HOSPITAL TANK** for proper setup.

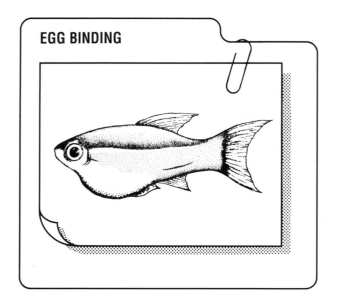

EGG BINDING

Egg binding can occur in freshwater fish during their spawning cycles. In their natural environment, a fish releases its eggs during the spawning cycle. However, if the fish cannot find a suitable mate, has been fed a poor diet, or if the tank or water conditions of the aquarium are not ideal for spawning, a fish may not be able to release its eggs. The result is a buildup of eggs, causing the fish to look bloated in the belly. The best prevention for egg binding is to maintain optimum water conditions (see **WATER CHEMISTRY**), and to make sure you are feeding your fish the proper diet for its species (see **FEEDING**).

When making a diagnosis of egg binding, be careful not to confuse egg binding with dropsy (see **DROPSY**). The main difference is that dropsy bloats the entire body, causing the scales to protrude from the fish's body, while egg-bound fish are bloated in the belly only. Also, egg binding is usually seen in freshwater aquarium fish only.

Symptoms: The fish is severely bloated in the belly only (not the whole body). The fish may also be lethargic, exhibit rapid breathing and have a loss of appetite.

Treatment: No medication is available for the treatment of egg binding. Attempts to squeeze the eggs from the body will usually damage the internal organs of the fish. Therefore, the only treatment for egg binding is to let the eggs be naturally absorbed into the fish's body. This process can be aided with magnesium sulfate (Epsom salt) soaks.

Siphon a bucket of tank water and mix in one slightly rounded tablespoon of Epsom salt for every one gallon of water. Add an airstone, place the fish in the water, cover the bucket and allow the fish a 15-minute soak. Repeat this treatment daily until the fish begins to recover.

In some cases, the eggs may bind the internal organs to the point of rupture. If this occurs, the fish will probably die. Therefore, if the fish is suffering greatly and its condition has deteriorated to probable death, you can try squeezing the eggs from the body. Net the fish and place it on a clean, wet towel. Insert a sterile needle just inside the fish's egg canal opening to help clear the passage. Place the belly of the fish between your forefinger and thumb and gently squeeze the eggs out of the fish. Considerable pressure may be needed to extract the eggs. You don't need to remove all the eggs, just enough to relieve the pressure. If at any time the intestines of the fish begin to protrude, stop immediately! Do not leave the fish out of the water for more than one minute.

Warning: The chance of this procedure being successful is limited, and the chance is great of killing the fish in the process. Therefore, squeezing the eggs from the fish should only be used as a last resort.

EXOTIC FISH

Exotic fish such as sharks, rays, skates, eels or seahorses offer beauty and additional interest to any marine aquarium. Special consideration should be given however, when keeping these fish. Listed below are the common problems, symptoms and treatments for these exotic fish.

EELS: Most of the problems with eels involve feeding, escaping from the aquarium or internal diseases and parasites.

Eels are highly successful as escape artists and can scale the sides or find an escape route out of any aquarium. If you have an eel, be sure that all lids are shut, weighted and all holes are filled. If you don't, your eel may greet you in the hallway some morning!

Feeding: Most eels are voracious eaters. Therefore, the feeding problem with eels is not in getting them to eat, but rather what they eat; namely tankmates.

Eels are nocturnal creatures that usually hide during the day and prowl at night. If there is no food for them during their prowl, they may be satisfied with a sleeping tankmate. Eels seem especially fond of eating cleaner shrimp and other crustaceans. To avoid this problem, add their favorite food to the aquarium just before turning off the room lights each evening. Eels are carnivores and should be fed strictly animal products such as crushed clams, shrimp, krill, squid or fish.

Diseases: Protozoan, fungal and fluke diseases are rarely a problem for eels. Eels also seem to be immune to marine Ick (Cryptocaryon). Therefore, diseased eels usually show no outwardly visible signs of disease as other fish do.

Symptoms: If your eel becomes lethargic, loses its appetite, breaths rapidly or begins to waste away, the eel is probably suffering from internal parasites. Usually the cause is a tapeworm or trematode attached to the kidneys, intestines or urinary bladder. Unfortunately, these parasites cannot be definitively diagnosed without a postmortem examination.

Treatment: Internal parasites in eels are best treated with Nitrofuran baths (see **Nitrofuran Bath** under **SHRIMP and LOBSTERS**, in **INVERTEBRATES**). Note that the dosage for eels should be 250 mg. of nitrofuran per gallon of water, not the recommended .5 grams for lobsters.

Medicated food should also be added to the diseased eel's diet as described in **CAMALLANUS WORMS**.

SEAHORSES: Seahorses can contract nearly all the diseases and have the same problems as marine fish. Seahorses can also receive wounds from aggressive fish, and they are especially prone to a buildup of gas in their pouches.

The slow swimming seahorse is nearly defenseless against an aggressive fish. In addition, seahorses only eat live food, and have a difficult time competing for food against fast swimming fish. Seahorses, then, should be kept in a tank separate from fish.

Feeding: Dwarf seahorses should be fed live, baby brine shrimp. Larger seahorses can be fed such foods as live brine shrimp, baby mollies or small guppies. If you are keeping seahorses, you should consider hatching and raising their food. If you depend on purchasing live food from fish dealers, there may be certain seasonal times that the dealer is out of live food. For instance, because of the increased baggage volume during the Christmas holidays, some airlines do not have any extra room, and will not allow items such as live fish on board for several days.

Water chemistry is the same for seahorses as for marine fish. Refer to **WATER CHEMISTRY** for proper requirements.

Symptoms/Treatment: It is more difficult to see signs of disease on a seahorse's skin than on a fish's skin. It is easier to discover signs of trouble on its tiny fins. Observe the fins closely for white spots, haziness or fraying. Since the seahorse can develop the same diseases as fish, use the **Fish Problems Flow Charts** to determine the problem, and treat accordingly.

Before you treat the seahorse for a bloated pouch, make sure it is not pregnant. If you have several seahorses, chances are it may be pregnant (the male carries the babies). If you have only one seahorse, or have not observed any mating, it is probably a gas bubble buildup. If the seahorse is distressed by the bubble, it should be treated.

Net the seahorse and place it on a clean, wet towel. Gently insert a sterilized, fine needle just inside the pouch opening to clear the passage. Then gently squeeze the gas from the pouch with your fingers. Dip a cotton swab in a broad spectrum antiseptic such as betadine (available at drug stores). Dab the pouch with the swab. Wait ten seconds for the antiseptic to penetrate, then place the seahorse directly into its tank. Do not keep the seahorse out of the water for more than one minute.

SHARKS, and RAYS (or SKATES): Proper water conditions are most important to this family of fish. Refer to **WATER CHEMISTRY** to ensure proper water conditions. Sharks and rays aren't as susceptible to as many diseases as other fish, but they tend to be prone to bacterial infections or gill and skin flukes.

Sharks and rays are also susceptible to shock caused from the stress of capture and transport. If one of these animals dies a few days after you have placed it in the tank, and the water conditions are ideal, the death is most likely due to shock.

Sharks will sometimes prowl, feed and fight at night. If you notice a fish missing or severely wounded some morning, it is most likely the result of a shark attack during the night.

Sharks have razor sharp teeth and are unpredictable at best, so be cautious. Some rays have electric or poisonous barbed tails but will only sting in self defense, so you should have no problem with them if you are careful. If you are ever bitten or stung by a shark or ray, seek medical attention immediately!

Water Sensitivity: Sharks and rays cannot tolerate any type of copper, nickel or other metal treatment or water contamination. If your main tank has ever been medicated with copper, some residual copper has most likely become bound in the gravel bottom or in carbonate base decorations such as tuffa rock or coral.

Before placing these fish in your tank, stir the gravel and thoroughly siphon all debris from the gravel bottom. Run the water through carbon power filters for several hours to help remove the copper. When placed in the tank, if the fish has a severe adverse reaction to the water, temporarily house it in freshly prepared saltwater (see **POISONING**). Stir the gravel, make a 50 percent water change, and run the water through carbon filtration again.

Feeding: Sharks and rays are strictly carnivores and should be fed animal foods only such as shrimp, fish, squid and krill. Rays are very fond of eating mollusks and crustaceans, so don't stock these animals with rays.

Rays do not have razor sharp teeth like sharks do. Their teeth are more flat and dull, and are used for crushing shells rather than ripping flesh. Therefore, feed smaller sized pieces of animal foods to rays.

It is advisable to avoid stocking the beautifully colored butterfly rays. These rays never seem to adapt to feeding in captivity and will eventually starve to death.

Diseases: Sharks and rays seem almost immune to marine Ick (Cryptocaryon) and other external protozoan and fungal diseases. Skin and gill flukes, and bacterial diseases are the most common problems in this family.

Although it is a sign of disease among bony fish, resting on the tank bottom does not indicate a problem for this group. The shark and ray family do not have swim bladders. This is why they sink to the bottom when they stop swimming.

Symptoms/Diagnosis: If rapid breathing and a lack of appetite is noticed with a shark or ray for more than two days, it probably indicates a bacterial infection.

Gill and skin flukes on sharks or rays are invisible to the aquarist. In addition, these fish will usually not show signs of most external diseases. This makes a diagnosis by observation alone nearly impossible. Therefore, when you suspect a disease with a shark or ray assume first that it has a bacterial cause. If the antibiotic treatment is unsuccessful, then treat for flukes.

Treatment: Bacterial infections among sharks and rays are best treated with nitrofuran baths (see **Nitrofuran Bath** under **SHRIMP and LOBSTERS, in INVERTEBRATES**). Note that the dosage for sharks and rays should be 250 mg. of nitrofuran per gallon of water, not the recommended .5 grams for lobsters.

If the fish does not respond to this treatment, treat for gill and skin flukes with trichlorfon or another anti-parasitic medication for use against anchor worms. Follow all manufacturer's directions. Never treat sharks or rays with copper!

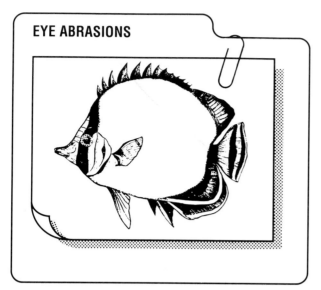

EYE ABRASIONS

The eyes of fish can be scratched by coarse nets, transport bags, or by fighting with aggressive fish, or swimming into objects when suddenly frightened. Eye abrasions are usually visible to an alert aquarist.

If an eye becomes hazy or cloudy after the fish has been recently netted or transported, it has probably been scratched. Remember to use fine mesh nets, a plastic bag or glass jar to capture fish. After use, always disinfect the net or jar in boiling water to control the spread of disease.

If the abrasion was caused by fighting, refer to **FIGHTING & FISH COMPATIBILITY** for future prevention.

Symptoms: The cornea is scratched, or the eye is hazy or cloudy (especially if the fish has been recently netted). No other symptoms of disease are present.

Treatment: For a minor abrasion, observe the eye for one day. If it begins to clear, no treatment is needed. If available, feed the fish prepackaged antibiotic medicated food as a preventative measure.

If the problem remains after one day, or if the condition worsens, net the fish and place it in the hospital tank. Refer to **HOSPITAL TANK** for proper setup. Treat the fish for five days with a broad spectrum antibiotic such as nitrofuran (furan). Follow the manufacturer's dosage directions.

Note: If you must treat the fish in the main tank, refer to **MAIN TANK MEDICATION**.

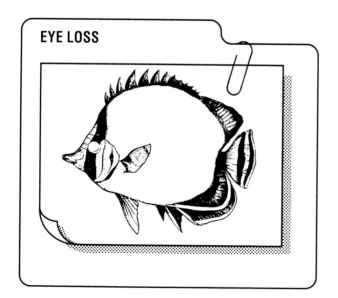

EYE LOSS

Occasionally, a fish may lose an eye from a severe case of a disease, such as popeye, or the eye may have been punctured from fighting or swimming into a sharp object. The eye may become completely detached from its socket, leaving the fish blind in that eye. The loss of an eye is not necessarily traumatic for the fish. Fish can live a relatively normal life with only one eye.

If the eye was lost because of disease, use the **Fish Problems Flow Charts** to make the correct diagnosis, and treat the fish accordingly.

Symptoms: The fish's eye detaches from its socket or is punctured. The fish may have depth perception problems when swimming or eating.

Treatment: Net the fish and place it on a clean, wet towel. Dip a cotton swab in a broad spectrum antibiotic such as betadine (available at drug stores). Dab the swab directly on the damaged eye, or in the empty eye socket. Let the drug penetrate for ten seconds, and then place the fish directly back in the main tank. Do not keep the fish out of the water for more than one minute.

If the eye loss has caused severe complications, you may need to consider a painless death for your fish. If this is the case, refer to **MERCY KILLING**.

Note: If you must treat the fish in the main tank, refer to **MAIN TANK MEDICATION**.

FEEDING

Most aquarists know the importance of proper feeding in order to maintain healthy fish, but what may not be obvious is what constitutes "proper" feeding. Proper feeding refers to providing the correct food for your species, supplying a varied diet, using the proper procedures and the right amount of food, as well as knowing how to feed sick, shy or troubled fish.

Proper Diet: Different species of fish have different food requirements. You need to use the right type of food for the particular species you are keeping. Feeding a carnivore (meat or insect eater) a strict diet of flakes will probably result in a weak, sluggish, dull-colored specimen, that is prone to disease. The same is true when feeding an herbivore (plant eater) only animal products. A summary of the food requirements for several different marine and freshwater species is at the end of this section.

Varied Diet: Feeding only one type of food, such as flakes, over an extended period of time, is just as unhealthy for fish as it would be for humans to eat only breakfast cereal. Fish fed only one type of food can develop constipation, diarrhea or even disease because the fish's resistance has been lowered due to poor nutrition. Fish should be fed varieties of food.

Think of the meat and vegetable food groups when choosing fish food. Flakes should be given along with a variety of food such as lettuce, green peas, brine shrimp or beef hearts. Ask your fish dealer about the different types of food available for your species. Most fish will enjoy the variety and even develop their favorite foods. Remember that a varied, healthy diet promotes bright colors, helps fight diseases, and keeps a fish's digestive organs "regular".

Serving Size: Proper feeding also means knowing the correct amount to feed. One of the easiest ways to poison a tank is to overfeed your fish. This is the most common problem among new aquarists. If you have a low volume tank (20 gallons or less), and your fish were fine yesterday but are dead today, the cause is probably toxicity from overfeeding. Large amounts of uneaten food left in the tank bottom quickly cause bacteria levels to rise, robbing the water of necessary oxygen. This can cause the fish to suffocate.

To avoid overfeeding, give your fish only small portions, and observe how much and how quickly they eat. A general rule is to feed no more than fish can eat in three minutes and observe their eating enthusiasm. If the fish still appear excited about eating, add a bit more food to the tank and once again observe their eating fervor. You should stop feeding just before the fish begin to lose interest in the food. A fish's appetite can vary daily, and this is why you should feed in small quantity successions. Most fish are satisfied after five to ten minutes of feeding. Feed twice daily, if possible, and remember to vary the diet.

Troublesome Eaters: Some fish can be quite troublesome to feed. A new fish may not eat for a few days; diseased fish may stop eating; other fish are shy and cannot compete with bullies for food; while other fish are just finicky eaters. It is up to you to determine which case applies to each troublesome eater. Use the **Fish Problems Flow Charts** to be sure that the fish is not diseased. If it is diseased, the proper cure is your concern; not feeding.

Healthy new fish that don't eat are either suffering from shock (see **SHOCK**), don't like the food, or don't realize it is a food source. If you vary the diet daily, you should quickly discover the type of food that your new fish prefers.

Bullies may take most of the food from timid fish. The best way to deal with a bully is to feed him his favorite food first. While feeding, observe how much the other fish are getting. When the bully is satisfied, feed the proper amount of the timid fish's favorite food. If your fish is extremely shy, you may have to place the food directly in front of him or separate the bully from the shy fish with a glass partition.

Nocturnal Fish: If your fish is a nocturnal species, there may be no food leftover for it to eat during the night. In this case, add a small amount of the nocturnal fish's favorite food to the tank just before you turn off the room lights. The next morning, observe to see if the food has been eaten. Be careful to feed very small amounts at night. You don't want to pollute the tank.

Vacation Feeding: Keeping your fish properly fed during vacations has always been a problem for the aquarist. As a general rule, if you will only be away for two to three days, your fish should be fine without any food. However, any longer than three days may result in the more aggressive fish making a meal out of some of their smaller tankmates.

There are a few options for proper vacation feeding, and each depends on how difficult your fish are to feed. If all of your fish will eat flakes, an electric, automatic fish feeder may be the answer. These feeders can be set to drop flakes into the tank twice a day for several weeks. There are also some products that slowly dissolve over several days, releasing food into the tank water. If your fish will eat live plants, purchase a few inexpensive plants for them to feed on as they become hungry. This is especially helpful during short, two-to three-day trips.

The best method for feeding fish during vacations is to use an automatic feeder to drop flake food into the tank, and have a trusted friend visit your home at least every other day. If even one of your fish won't eat anything but live or daily prepared food, you will need to have a friend, fish dealer, or house sitter feed your fish.

Have individual packets of food already prepared with the proper portions so your friend needs only to drop the contents into the tank. Before you leave, instruct your friend how to properly feed the fish. In addition, have this manual handy, and show him/her how to give the fish and the entire system a quick check for any problems (see **WATER CHEMISTRY**). Let him/her know how to contact you or a local expert (a trusted hobbyist or fish dealer) if there are any emergencies while you're away. Also, leave a phone number where you can be reached in an emergency.

Fish Wasting Away: If you have a fish that eats but is still losing weight, is pinched in the belly or wasting away, it is probably suffering from tuberculosis or some internal disease or parasite. Use the **Fish Problems Flow Charts** to make a proper diagnosis and treat accordingly.

Proper Feeding Procedures Summary: Feed small quantities of food to determine how hungry the fish are. Give the correct food for the species and provide a varied diet. Feed twice a day. Feed bullies first, and if necessary, feed troublesome eaters separately. Thaw frozen food in a cup of tank water first, then pour it into the tank. Don't shake flake food from its container, instead, take a pinch with your fingers and place it into the tank water. Siphon or net and remove any uneaten food.

Proper Foods for Freshwater and Marine Fish: Fish can be classified in three categories of feeders: carnivores (meat or fly eaters), herbivores (plant eaters), or omnivores (both plant and meat eaters). Be sure to feed your fish their staple food and vary their diet with foods from the other categories. Be careful when feeding live foods, since they can transmit many diseases to the aquarium. Never feed live food from ponds or streams. Instead, raise your own live foods.

Be experimental with feeding. Ask your fish dealer about the many varieties of foods and occasionally add aquarium approved vitamins and minerals to the food or tank water. Most of your fish will enjoy the variety and thrive because of the nutritional benefits.

Listed below are the feeding categories for fish. This list is to be used as a general guideline only. You should research the feeding habits of your specific fish. As a general rule, consider all fish carnivores, and supplement herbivores with plant and vegetable foods.

Carnivores: Freshwater carnivores include snakeheads, Jack Dempseys, piranhas, archerfish, gobies, hatchetfish, knifefish, arowanas, tetras and angelfish. Marine carnivores include triggerfish, lionfish, anglerfish, squirrelfish, clowns, groupers, cowfish, damselfish, butterflyfish, angelfish and even sea horses.

Carnivores should be fed a staple food of animal products, and their diet should be varied with flakes and herbivore plant and vegetable foods. Animal foods include brine shrimp, beef hearts, small feeder fish, freeze dried tubifex (worms) or mosquitoes. A marine carnivore diet could also include finely chopped crustaceans and krill.

Herbivores: Freshwater herbivores include tilapias, and banded leporinus. Marine herbivores include wrasses, surgeonfish and tangs.

Herbivores should be fed carnivore staple foods and flakes, and supplemented with equal amounts of algae, one finely chopped lettuce and/or spinach leaf, thawed green peas, and whole leaf romaine lettuce. Place one romaine lettuce leaf on a plastic two-inch pipe and secure it to the pipe with a rubber band. Attach a fish line to the pipe for easy retrieval, then lower it into the tank. Many herbivores will also eat the vegetable food pellets manufactured for guinea pigs.

Omnivores: Freshwater omnivores include goldfish, cichlids, oscars, barbs, scats, gouramis, loaches, mollies, fighting bettas, catfish, puffers, and swordtails. Marine omnivores include box or trunkfish, puffers, blennies, and batfish. Omnivores should be fed carnivore foods supplemented with flakes and herbivore plant and vegetable foods.

FIGHTING & FISH COMPATIBILITY

Fish are territorial creatures. In their natural habitat, fish have their own food source and shelter, which they will defend from roving scavengers. In the confines of an aquarium, a fish's territory becomes more difficult to defend. This is especially true if the tank tends to be overcrowded. In addition, it is much more difficult for a timid fish to escape a bully in an aquarium. Because of this, there will occasionally be some nipped fins, fighting or even killing among your fish and aquatic animal collection.

If you have a community tank, it is likely there will be one fish that is the "boss" of the tank. Ironically, the boss may not even be the largest fish, just the most aggressive. The boss will chase away any fish that comes near its territory. It may even take a stand against you when you are cleaning the tank. Removing the boss is sometimes only a temporary solution to the problem. Once that fish is gone, another fish may soon take the role of "tank boss". There are, however, a few alternatives that will reduce the bickering in a community tank.

The primary cause of fighting among fish is incompatibility. Placing an aggressive fish with a docile, weak swimmer in a small aquarium, sentences the timid fish to a life of being chased and a probable fatal beating.

Rule one, when selecting fish, is to carefully choose compatible tankmates. Avoid selecting more than one of the same type of fish. Fish of the same species compete for the same food, swim in the same space, and search for the same type of shelter. They are constant competitors for every necessity of life. This can lead to many "scraps" within the confines of a tank. This is especially true among marine fish or in small, overcrowded freshwater aquariums.

Don't choose fish that are all bottom feeders, all surface feeders, all the same color, or all the same size. On the other hand, be aware that a very small fish is no match for a large aggressor. Choose one or two from each category and give your community tank a variety of fish. Your fish dealer should be able to provide guidance regarding fish compatibility when selecting your community fish.

Rule number two, for fish compatibility, is to provide as much space to swim and as many various forms of shelter as possible (see **Overcrowding** in **WATER CHEMISTRY**). Every fish should have space to swim, and a shelter for safety when frightened.

Rule number three is to feed your fish a variety of food, and make sure the fish are being fed the correct amount and type of food for their particular species (see **FEEDING**). Fish that eat different foods won't fight for the same morsel of food.

If you follow these rules, yet acts of aggressiveness, fighting and nipped fins are still occurring, you have a bully! This may be especially true if there has been a new addition to the tank. Temporarily separate the bully from the rest of its tankmates, using a glass partition. In an emergency, the glass tank top lid can be used temporarily. Place a towel over the tank so the fish can't jump out. This will give the bully a few days to get used to the new fish without being able to attack it.

After a few days, remove the glass and observe the interaction. If chasing continues for more than a few hours, rearrange all of the tank rocks, coral and decorations. It is important to rearrange the entire tank. This confuses the bully, who no longer has a favorite territory to defend.

This rearrangement is also very effective in controlling a fish that is picking on invertebrates, or is constantly destructive to the tank's landscaping. It should take a few days for new territories to be established. If the bullying continues, decide which fish you want to keep; the other one must go!

Don't destroy the unwanted fish. Place it in a heavyweight plastic bag half filled with tank water and half with air, and present your favorite fish dealer with another fish to sell. Hopefully, your fish will find a happier home, and maybe your dealer will return the favor in the future.

For treatment of wounds caused by fighting, see **FISH FIRST AID**.

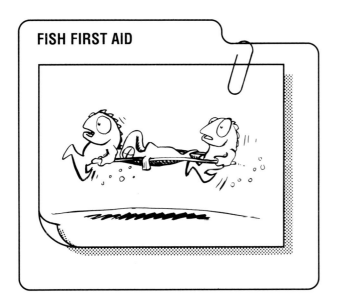

Fish can be wounded by aggressive tank mates, stung by poisonous fish or anemones, or injure themselves by scraping against a sharp piece of rock or coral when suddenly frightened. There are three immediate concerns when a fish is injured: the severity of the injury, aggressive tank mates and a possible secondary bacterial or fungal infection.

The severity of the injury can be determined by how the fish behaves. If it has been wounded but still eats and swims normally, assume that it is not a serious injury. If the fish hides, has trouble swimming or defending itself, or suddenly does not eat, it is a serious injury. Knowing the severity of the injury determines the length of time needed for treatment. If the fish's wound has caused a severe breathing problem or if it is hyperventilating, artificial respiration may be needed (see **ARTIFICIAL RESPIRATION**).

Prevention of wounds is most easily achieved when the tankmates are compatible and the fish are not suddenly frightened. Fish can be frightened by someone turning on the aquarium light in a dark room, by someone banging on the tank glass or from being chased by an aggressor. If fighting is the cause, see **FIGHTING & FISH COMPATIBILITY** in this manual for prevention.

<u>Symptoms:</u> The fish's fins are nipped (from fighting, not fin rot). Cuts, scrapes or stings are on its body, and the fish may also be bleeding, hiding, swimming limply or not eating.

<u>Treatment:</u> Net the fish and place it on a clean, wet towel. Dip a cotton swab in a broad spectrum antiseptic such as betadine (available at drug stores). Dab the swab on the wounded area of the fish's skin. Let the drug penetrate for ten seconds then immediately return the fish to the main tank. Don't keep the fish out of the water for more than one minute.

A seriously wounded fish is easy prey for an aggressive tankmate. Therefore, prepare the hospital tank for severely injured fish. See **HOSPITAL TANK** for the proper setup. If you can't immediately prepare the hospital tank, separate the injured fish from any aggressive fish using a glass partition or glass tank lid.

If the fish has deep cuts or abrasions, net the fish with a soft mesh net or plastic bag and treat it with betadine as described above. Place the fish in the hospital tank. Ask your fish dealer to recommend a proper (marine or freshwater) broad spectrum antibiotic manufactured for the prevention of secondary bacterial or fungal infections such as nitrofuran (see **BACTERIAL INFECTION**). Follow the manufacturer's dosage recommendations. For minor injuries, recovery should be complete within one week. Severely injured fish should be treated until they begin to show normal swimming and eating patterns.

If the fish has been severely injured or stung, it may not recover. If you determine that the fish will not survive, a quick, painless death may be necessary. If this is the case, refer to **MERCY KILLING**.

Note: If you must treat the fish in the main tank, refer to **MAIN TANK MEDICATION**.

One of the most frustrating experiences you may face as a fish hobbyist is having fish die with no apparent sign of problems or disease. When this happens, it may be nearly impossible to determine exactly what is going wrong inside your aquarium.

A small percentage of the marine fish that are caught in the Philippines are still being captured with the use of cyanide. Cyanide has a delayed effect on the fish that can cause them to die suddenly, a few days after arrival. Cyanide laden fish tend to have intense colorations. Ask your fish dealer where the fish are from and how they were caught.

New fish added to the tank can also die from unusual stress caused from capture and transport (see **SHOCK**). Many of the new additions are also carriers of disease which explains why a new outbreak of Ick or another disease sometimes occurs just after a recent addition. The best way to avoid the introduction of disease into your tank is to have a quarantine tank (see **Quarantine Tank** in **HOSPITAL TANK**) to hold a new fish for a two-week observation period before placing it in the main tank.

If several new fish have died without a visible sign of the cause, it is likely that you have a problem with water conditions. Refer to **WATER CHEMISTRY**, and pay particular attention to Ammonia, Nitrites & the Biological Filter, Overcrowding, Temperature and Aeration. Remember, if you have a new, non-established tank, adding just one fish can affect the biological balance of the aquarium. Therefore, gradually space the additions of any new fish by several days to several weeks.

New aquarists tend to overfeed their fish. The uneaten food decays, causing a rapid buildup of bacteria, depleting oxygen and eventually suffocating the fish. If you have a small tank and the fish appeared fine yesterday but are dead today, the problem is most likely toxicity caused from overfeeding. Refer to **FEEDING** for overfeeding prevention.

Another cause of death to new fish is starvation. If the fish is not eating, see **Troublesome Eaters** in **FEEDING**.

Remember that fish can also die natural deaths. If you have had a fish for a few years and noticed no symptoms of disease or tank trouble either just before or after its death, your fish may have died a natural death.

Treatment: When several fish are dying in an established tank without any signs of disease, and the water conditions are normal, a disease or parasite may be present, but still invisible to you, and is randomly attacking your fish. The best solution would be to find a veterinarian in your area that can perform a postmortem on a fish that has recently died. If this is not possible, you have no choice but to treat all your fish for the major diseases.

Treat your fish first for Invisible Ick according to **ICK**. If this treatment is not successful, treat according to **BACTERIAL INFECTION**. If both treatments are unsuccessful assume an internal disease is present and treat the fish according to **CAMALLANUS WORMS**. If several new, small, freshwater fish have died, treat your fish according to **FUNGUS**.

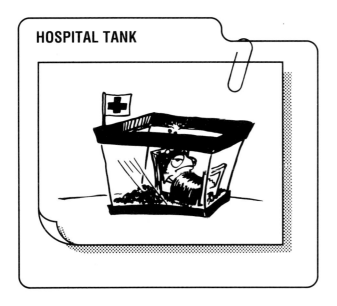

There are several reasons why a hospital tank should be used to treat diseased fish, rather than treating them in the main tank. First, many drugs will harm, if not kill, the beneficial bacteria that lives in the gravel bottom of an aquarium and serves as the natural biological filter. If a significant amount of the bacteria dies, you may have to begin the biological filter cycle of the main tank all over again, which could mean the death of some of your more delicate species (see **POISONING**).

Second, aquatic medicine can often be expensive. If you have a rather large show tank (over 40 gallons), you would need eight times the amount of medicine than with a five-gallon hospital tank. The costs for medicine for as few as three treatments in the main tank would exceed the cost of the hospital tank. You may be using the hospital tank quite a few times so it is money well spent.

Third, treating fish in a main tank means you'll be medicating all of the healthy fish as well. It is not wise to give drugs to delicate, healthy fish.

Finally, sick fish tend to hide. A separate, smaller tank is much easier to control and monitor the conditions, progress, and recovery of your fish.

The recommended hospital tank size is five gallons (unless you have unusually large fish). A tank this small is easier to store, handle, move, clean and monitor. Purchase a tank complete with lid, heater and thermometer.

Follow these steps to get the hospital tank in operation:

1. Clean and rinse all equipment and utensils to be used, with hot, fresh water only.

2. Place the hospital tank on a sturdy stand next to the main tank, if possible.

3. Fill the hospital tank by siphoning five gallons of water from the main tank. Be sure to replace the five gallons of water from the main tank.

4. Bleed air from the main tank's air pump into the hospital tank by use of a gang valve. Attach an airstone to the end of the tubing.

5. If possible, place the heater in the middle of the hospital tank to evenly disperse the heat. Adjust the heater to maintain the same temperature as the main tank.

6. Provide a shelter in the hospital tank for the fish. A small clay flower pot works quite well. Purchase several flower pots of different sizes and choose one the size of the quarantined fish. Rinse the pot with hot, fresh water and place it on its side in the hospital tank.

7. Medicate the tank according to the pharmaceutical manufacturer's recommendations for five gallons.

8. With a fine mesh net, remove the affected fish from the main tank and place it in the hospital tank, allowing it a few minutes to calm down. If you have difficulty catching the fish, you may have to remove some of the decorations from one side to corral the fish.

9. Keep the hospital tank dark. This is necessary because some diseases need light to survive, the strength of some drugs decreases when exposed to light, and low light is less stressful on the fish. If you can't keep the room dark, place a towel or paper bag around the tank.

10. Increase aeration in the hospital tank. The reason for this is that many medications deplete oxygen from the water. Also, diseased fish often have trouble breathing. If the instructions on the medication recommend it, adjust the temperature to the indicated higher setting at this time.

Now that the hospital tank is in operation, follow these steps throughout the treatment period:

1. **Feeding:** Sick fish usually eat very little food, and very sick fish won't eat at all. The first day, don't feed the sick fish anything. The second and remaining days, feed only half of the fish's normal portion. This is because a five-gallon tank can quickly become polluted from uneaten food or waste.

2. **Daily Observation:** Observe the fish closely for signs of improvement, deterioration or other symptoms. Also, closely monitor the temperature in the hospital tank since a faulty thermostat can quickly raise the temperature in a five-gallon tank.

   If, at any time, the fish has a sudden, adverse reaction to the medication, quickly siphon as much water from the hospital tank as possible and refill it with water from the main tank. Return to your fish dealer and purchase a different drug recommended for the particular disease.

   Monitor the ammonia levels of the hospital tank daily. Ammonia levels can rise quickly to lethal levels in a five-gallon tank. This especially true if you have a large fish in quarantine. If ammonia levels are high, a 100 percent water change is needed (see Water Replacement section, which follows).

3. **Water Replacement:** Every other day, unplug the heater in the hospital tank and siphon the tank bottom to remove the excess food and waste. Using a pail that has gallon markings, siphon exactly two-and one-half gallons of water. Dispose of the used water.

Next, siphon two-and one-half gallons of water from the main tank into the hospital tank. Plug in the heater. Now re-medicate the hospital tank with one-half the recommended dosage for five-gallons.

When the following conditions are present, a complete water change is required each day as described below.

- Ammonia levels are high. This can happen quickly in a five-gallon tank, especially if you have a large fish in quarantine.

- Tetracycline or malachite green is used. Drugs such as these break down completely in 24 to 48 hours.

- Copper is used. The copper ion level needs to be maintained at a rate of .25 ppm in order to remain effective.

Siphon as much water from the hospital tank as possible into a bucket with graduation markings. Refill the tank with siphoned main tank water and re-medicate proportionally to the amount of water extracted. Replace the water taken from the main tank.

Continue procedures one, two and three throughout the treatment period.

When your fish has recovered, follow these steps to dismantle the hospital tank:

- With a fine mesh net, remove the fish from the hospital tank and place it directly in the main tank.

- Unplug the hospital tank's heater.

- Remove the airstone and tubing from the hospital tank. Siphon and dispose of the used water.

- Using hot, fresh water, thoroughly clean all equipment and utensils, including nets.

Quarantine Tank: The hospital tank should also be used as a quarantine for any new specimens you purchase. Diseased fish sometimes do not show visible symptoms for several days. If you place new fish or animals directly into the main tank immediately after purchase, and if the fish is diseased, it may infect other tankmates as well. Be patient. Keep all new arrivals for two weeks in the quarantine tank.

To quarantine new fish, use these steps:

1. Follow instructions one through six for hospital tank setup.

2. Don't place a new fish directly into the quarantine tank. Leave it in the transport bag. Wipe the outside of the bag clean with a damp cloth, open the bag and float it in the quarantine tank for 40 minutes.

3. Keep the room dark to help ease the shock of transport.

4. Every ten minutes, add about one cup of tank water to the water in the plastic bag. This will help the new fish slowly become accustomed to the chemistry of the quarantine tank's water.

5. When 40 minutes have passed, remove the fish from the plastic bag with a fine mesh net, and place it in the quarantine tank. Never pour the water from the plastic bag directly into the quarantine tank because it may contain some form of disease or toxin.

6. During the two week quarantine:

    • Add no medication.

    • Monitor ammonia levels daily.

    • Make a 50 percent water change every other day.

    • Feed one-half portion of the fish's staple food.

    • Observe the fish closely for any signs of disease. If a problem is discovered, use the flow charts to make the proper diagnosis and treat accordingly.

INVERTEBRATES

Many marine and freshwater aquarists are venturing into stocking invertebrates in their aquariums. The unusual characteristics of the invertebrates add additional interest and beauty to any aquarium. However, when problems occur among invertebrates, they can be most difficult to remedy. Listed below are the problems, symptoms and treatments for the majority of invertebrates being kept by fish hobbyists.

ANEMONES: Problem indicators for anemones include: releasing its base from the point of attachment and not reattaching to a new structure, the ballooning of its base, degeneration of its tentacles, loss of coloration, shriveling in size or decaying, causing foul smelling water. Most problems with anemones are caused by inadequate lighting, poor nutrition or improper water conditions. In addition, secondary bacterial, fungal or protozoan infections can occur in wounds caused by rough handling or aggressive fish.

Symptoms/Diagnosis: If your anemone has lost its color or is shriveling, the cause is probably poor lighting or poor nutrition. If it has detached itself from its point of attachment and is floating around the tank, or if its base is bloated, the probable cause is improper water conditions. Wounds and abrasions usually cause visible secondary infections and decomposition.

If you have a new anemone that dies within a few days, even though lighting, feeding and water conditions are ideal, the anemone was probably damaged or poisoned by polluted water during transport to your fish dealer. If the anemone has an adverse reaction immediately after being placed in the aquarium, or if you have had the anemone for several weeks before any symptoms were noticed, the problem is most likely within your tank.

Lighting: Anemones have different lighting requirements than fish. Anemones require low intensity blue/green and red light. Therefore, normal aquarium lighting may not be sufficient for some anemones. If the anemone begins to degenerate, or if it loses its color, the problem is most likely caused by inadequate lighting.

The light requirements for anemones can be met by using an actinic 20 watt fluorescent light bulb. This bulb will require a different ballast than your aquarium strip light. Both the bulb and ballast are usually available from an electrical or specialty lighting store. Place the light on the aquarium glass lid directly over the anemone. Leave the actinic bulb on for at least 12 hours a day, regardless of how long you leave on the aquarium light.

A halide lamp can also be used for anemones, but the heat from the lamp tends to raise the tank water temperature. Therefore, halide lamps should only be used on deeper tanks.

Nutrition: Anemones should be fed animal products such as chopped fish, whole brine shrimp, or krill. In addition, liquid food specially packaged for invertebrates should be used as a dietary supplement. If the anemone is not getting enough to eat, the food should be placed directly in the mouth of the anemone with the use of plastic forceps.

Water Conditions: Water condition requirements for anemones are no different than for marine fish. Refer to **WATER CHEMISTRY** to determine if there is a problem.

Aggressive Fish: See **FIGHTING & FISH COMPATIBILITY** if an aggressive fish is causing trouble for the anemone. If the anemone has stung a fish, refer to **FISH FIRST AID** for the treatment of the fish.

Treatment: When the lighting, nutrition and/or water conditions are not ideal, correcting the improper condition will most likely solve the anemone's problem. If the above conditions are met, but the anemone has decomposition, it can be treated with freshwater baths.

Freshwater Baths: Prepare a clean bucket with one gallon of fresh tap water that is the same temperature as the tank water. Use dechlorination chemicals, available at your fish dealer, to remove the chlorine from the water. Wear plastic gloves to protect yourself from being stung, then gently remove the anemone from its point of attachment and place it in the bucket. Quickly, but gently, run your fingers over the tentacles and body, rubbing away the decomposition. Do not leave the anemone in the fresh water for more than two minutes. Gently swirl the anemone in the bucket of water as a rinse and then place it directly back into the main tank. Discard the bucket of water. Repeat once a day, as needed, for up to one week.

If this treatment is unsuccessful, anemones (anemones only) can be treated with nitrofuran baths. Refer to **Nitrofuran Bath** under **SHRIMP and LOBSTERS** below. Change the dosage to one gram of nitrofuran per gallon of water for anemones instead of the .5 grams recommended for lobsters. **Warning:** Never use drugs in the presence of live coral, sea fans or sponges!

LIVE CORAL, SEA FANS and SPONGES: Problems with soft coral and sponges usually include degenerative diseases, loss of color, and grayish, slimy, soft or stubby tentacles. If a problem is discovered, it can consume the entire coral within one week.

Corals and sponges require the same lighting and water conditions as anemones. Liquid food should be provided that is specially manufactured for invertebrates (particularly true for sponges).

Treatment: If a problem is noticed just as the disease begins, the piece of the degenerating finger can be cut off and discarded. If this does not help, or if the disease has spread, treatment should be a freshwater bath described in **ANEMONES**. **Warning:** Never use drugs in the presence of live coral, sea fans, or sponges!

SHRIMP, LOBSTERS, CRABS and STARFISH: The majority of problems among these animals are loss of a limb, skin abrasions, the skin develops white patches, bacterial diseases, or the animal being "picked on" by aggressive fish during molting (shedding).

Molting: Periodically, crustaceans will shed their shell while they are rejuvenating a new one. This is a normal growth function, and is known as molting. During this period, the animals are left temporarily unprotected from other aggressive fish.

Signs are given by shrimps, crabs and lobsters just prior to molting, which an alert aquarist can recognize, and then react by moving the animal to a safe place. If the animal's normally black eyes become white, cloudy or hazy, and the animal stops feeding, it will probably molt within three to seven days. If these signs are noticed, remove it from the main tank and place it in a separate quarantine tank until it molts. See **HOSPITAL TANK** for proper setup. Any loss of limb among crustaceans and starfish requires no action, since the lost limb will rejuvenate itself after the next molt.

Symptoms/Treatment: Symptoms of disease among crustaceans and starfish include the skin developing white patches, or a pinkish coloration underneath the shrimp or lobster's tail. Either sign indicates a bacterial infection. Although medications have had limited success among diseased invertebrates, nitrofuran baths have proven to be a successful treatment.

Nitrofuran Bath: Visit your fish dealer and purchase an antibacterial medication that contains nitrofuran (or furan) in as pure a form as possible (no other drugs present). Fill a clean bucket with one gallon of siphoned tank water. Bleed the air from the air pump to the bucket using a gang valve. Attach the air tube to an airstone and place the stone in the bucket. Medicate the one gallon of water with .5 grams (.02 ounces) of nitrofuran. Place the animal in the bucket for 30 minutes and observe it closely.

After 30 minutes, if the animal appears weak, stressed or distressed, remove it from the bucket and place it directly back into the main tank. If it does not have an adverse reaction, leave it in the bucket for another 30 minutes before placing it in the main tank. Discard the medicated water. Repeat the treatment once a day for seven days.

If treatment is unsuccessful, and the animal is degenerating further, repeat the treatment and increase the dosage to one gram of nitrofuran per gallon of water. This increased dosage treatment should only be used as a last resort.

SNAILS: Many freshwater aquarists stock snails in their aquarium to help with tank cleaning maintenance. Snails are also sensitive to water chemistry, making them good early warning indicators of improper water conditions. However, snails can quickly overrun an aquarium if their population is not kept under control.

Symptoms: Problem signs include: the snails stop eating the algae from the tank glass, are unusually sluggish, lie on the tank bottom or withdraw into their shell.

Treatment: The above symptoms are caused by improper water conditions. Refer to **WATER CHEMISTRY** to determine the problem. If several snails have suddenly died, there is probably a toxin in the tank (see **POISONING**).

If the tank is being overrun by snails, manually remove as many of them as possible. If several snails have attached themselves to a plant or object, it may be easier to temporarily remove the object than to pick each snail off, while the object is in the tank. In fact, a routine thinning is a good way to keep the population under control.

With a rubber band, secure a lettuce or spinach leaf to a clean two-inch plastic pipe. Tie fish line around the pipe for easy retrieval, and place the pipe in the tank for a few hours, letting the snails collect on it. Remove the pipe by pulling on the fish line, and discard the lettuce leaf and snails. Don't use anti-snail medications unless you have severe snail overpopulation problems. Perform bi-weekly thinnings of the remaining stock to keep the snail population under control.

OCTOPUSES, SQUID, CUTTLEFISH and SEA SLUGS: Often, many of the problems with mollusks occur while they are still in their natural environment. In many cases, internal worms and flukes enter their bodies and attack their kidneys and other internal organs. These worms may be eating away at the internal organs while the animal shows no visible outward signs of problems or stress. Other problems may be caused by curious or aggressive fish. If fish are bothering your mollusks, see **FIGHTING & FISH COMPATIBILITY**.

Octopuses are highly successful as escape artists and can scale the sides of any aquarium. If you have an octopus, be sure that all lids are closed, weighted and all holes are filled. If you don't, your octopus may greet you in the hallway some morning!

Remember also, that most mollusks will only live two to three years, and dwarf octopuses live only one year. If the animal has no visible symptoms of abnormalities, but becomes sluggish, loses its appetite and dies, it probably has died from natural causes.

Symptoms/Diagnosis: If the mollusk has signs of rapid breathing, hyperactivity, or has become pale in color, the animal is probably infected with an internal parasitic disease. If the animal also becomes lethargic and loses its appetite, it will most likely die within two days.

Treatment: By the time the animal has shown visible signs of problems, it is probably too heavily infected to recover. However, at the first signs of trouble you could try treating the animal according to **CAMALLANUS WORMS**. Be sure to treat the animal in a separate hospital tank and feed the medicated food mentioned. Refer to **HOSPITAL TANK** for proper setup.

Warning: Some mollusks can squirt ink when threatened or affected by disease. The ink is extremely toxic, and can kill all the fish in your tank, including the mollusk. Therefore, if your animal shows any signs of trouble, move it to a separate hospital tank. Refer to **HOSPITAL TANK** for proper setup. If your animal has inked the tank, take immediate action according to **POISONING**, or it can kill all the fish, animals and plants in the tank!

SEA CUCUMBERS and SEA APPLES: These more exotic animals require the same water and lighting conditions as anemones. The food requirements are the same as that of live sponges. The majority of problems for these animals are caused by improper water conditions, improper feeding, abrasions or wounds from rough handling, aggressive fish, and/or disease.

Symptoms/Treatment: Sea cucumbers and sea apples possess extremely potent toxins which they release if diseased or wounded. If you notice any abnormality at all, the animal should be immediately removed from the tank. If its condition is severe, it should be discarded.

If the problem appears to be minor, try treating the animal by immediately placing it in a separate hospital tank (see **HOSPITAL TANK**). Medicate the hospital tank with a broad spectrum antibiotic medication that contains the drug nitrofuran. Follow all manufacturer's directions. Leave it in the hospital tank until it fully recovers. If your animal has poisoned your tank, take immediate action according to **POISONING**, or you will surely lose your entire stock of fish, animals and plants!

FLOW CHART INSTRUCTIONS

1. Begin at "START"
Always begin at "start" on the first flow chart. If you skip indiscriminately to other flow charts you could easily reach the wrong diagnosis.

2. Answer "Yes" or "No"
Carefully read all questions or statements, and then, concentrating on the primary symptom of your problem, answer with either "Yes" or "No". In the case of multiple symptoms, the primary symptom is that which is causing the most distress to your fish.

3. Reach the Diagnosis
Follow the appropriate arrows to the next box on the chart, and continue this procedure until you end at a symbol of a notebook or file folder. A notebook symbol 🗒 is used when the instructions can be briefly stated in the flowchart. A file folder symbol 🗀 means that you should refer to the manual for detailed instructions about the indicated diagnosis. If more than one diagnosis is shown, administer treatment in the order listed.

4. Double Check
Once you've reached the diagnosis, write it down. Then go back to step one and repeat the flow chart diagnosis process again. If you arrive at the same conclusion the second time, you have reached the most likely diagnosis for the problem.

BE SURE TO NOTE THE FOLLOWING:

5. When to Jump
All **"GO TO"** arrows indicate that you should ignore the rest of the flow chart that you are currently using and immediately jump to the first box of the named flow chart.

6. Let Symbols be Your Guide
The manual is divided into **GENERAL PROBLEMS, FISH DISEASES** and **EQUIPMENT PROBLEMS**. File folders that are darkened and have the microscope symbol 🔬 indicate that they are in the section for **FISH DISEASES**.

7. Try, Try Again
If you have used the flow charts properly and have treated the fish according to the manual, but the treatment has been unsuccessful, the diagnosis was probably incorrect. Carefully observe again to make sure you have not missed an important secondary symptom. Now, return to **"START"** on the first flow chart and proceed through the flow charts as before. This time, however, ignore your first diagnosis, and continue on through the flow chart until you reach a second, different diagnosis. Treat the fish accordingly.

START

NOTE:
Read detailed instructions before you start!

START HERE

The problem is with the live aquarium plants. — Yes → **PLANTS**

No ↓

The tank has algae problems. — Yes → **ALGAE CONTROL**

No ↓

There are fish feeding problems, troublesome eaters or problems feeding the fish during vacations. — Yes → **FEEDING**

No ↓

A fish dies, or several new fish die with no detectable symptoms. — Yes → **HIGH MORTALITY RATE**

No ↓

The problem is with a shark, ray, skate, eel, or seahorse. — Yes → **EXOTIC FISH**

No ↓

The problem is with a shrimp, lobster, live coral, live sea fan, live sponge, starfish, sea cucumber, sea apple, snail, octopus, squid, sea slug, cuttlefish or anemone. — Yes → **INVERTEBRATES**

No ↓

There are equipment problems, power outages, or water temperature problems. — Yes → GO TO **EQUIPMENT PROBLEMS**

No ↓

The problem is with a fish. — Yes → GO TO **FISH BREATHING PROBLEMS**

No ↓

You notice problems with the tank water. — Yes → GO TO **POISONING**

No ↓

NOTE: If a definitive diagnosis cannot be made, observe the fish, animal, equipment or source of trouble for other visible symptoms or contact your fish dealer or fish veterinarian.

INSTRUCTIONS SUMMARY
1. Always begin at **START**.
2. Answer **YES** or **NO** and follow the arrows.
3. Reach the diagnosis file.
4. Double check.
5. Refer to named file in manual.

NOTE: See detailed flow chart instructions on previous page.

KEY

- Question or statement box.
- **GO TO** the named flow chart.
- Refer to the named file under **GENERAL PROBLEMS** in manual.
- Refer to the named file under **FISH DISEASES** in manual.
- Equipment Problems flow chart.
- Fish Problems flow charts.
- Water Problems flow chart.
- Poisoning flow chart.
- Notes

EQUIPMENT

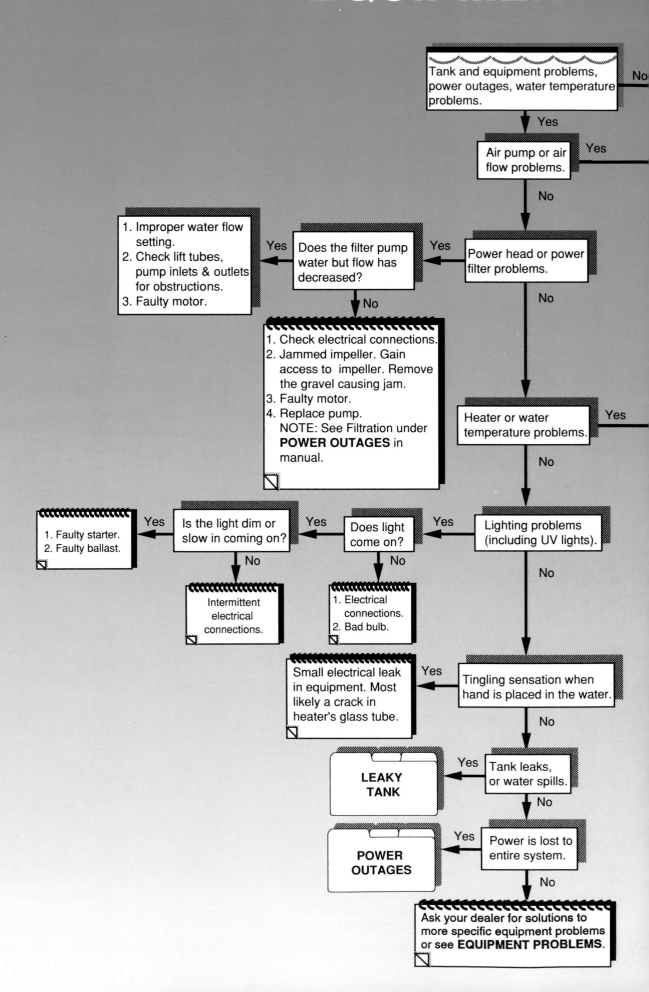

Tank and equipment problems, power outages, water temperature problems. — **No**

Yes ↓

Air pump or air flow problems. — **Yes**

No ↓

Power head or power filter problems. — **Yes** → Does the filter pump water but flow has decreased? — **Yes** →
1. Improper water flow setting.
2. Check lift tubes, pump inlets & outlets for obstructions.
3. Faulty motor.

No ↓ (from filter pump question)
1. Check electrical connections.
2. Jammed impeller. Gain access to impeller. Remove the gravel causing jam.
3. Faulty motor.
4. Replace pump.
NOTE: See Filtration under **POWER OUTAGES** in manual.

No ↓ (from power head)

Heater or water temperature problems. — **Yes**

No ↓

Lighting problems (including UV lights). — **Yes** → Does light come on? — **Yes** → Is the light dim or slow in coming on? — **Yes** →
1. Faulty starter.
2. Faulty ballast.

Is the light dim or slow in coming on? — **No** → Intermittent electrical connections.

Does light come on? — **No** →
1. Electrical connections.
2. Bad bulb.

No ↓ (from lighting)

Tingling sensation when hand is placed in the water. — **Yes** → Small electrical leak in equipment. Most likely a crack in heater's glass tube.

No ↓

Tank leaks, or water spills. — **Yes** → **LEAKY TANK**

No ↓

Power is lost to entire system. — **Yes** → **POWER OUTAGES**

No ↓

Ask your dealer for solutions to more specific equipment problems or see **EQUIPMENT PROBLEMS**.

PROBLEMS

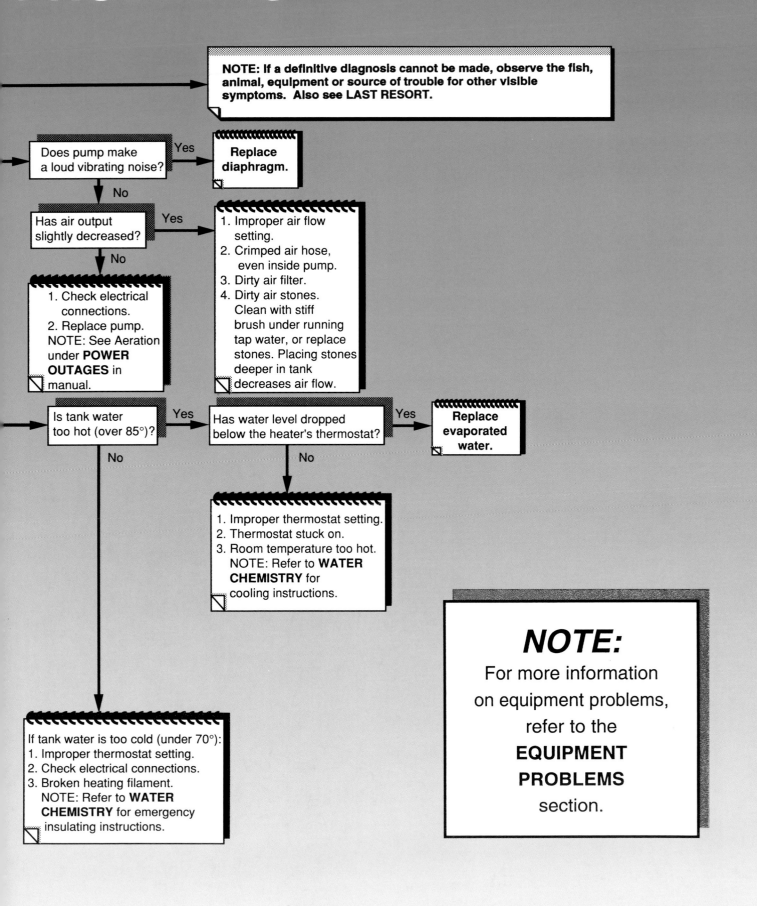

NOTE: If a definitive diagnosis cannot be made, observe the fish, animal, equipment or source of trouble for other visible symptoms. Also see LAST RESORT.

Does pump make a loud vibrating noise? — Yes → **Replace diaphragm.**

No ↓

Has air output slightly decreased? — Yes → 1. Improper air flow setting.
2. Crimped air hose, even inside pump.
3. Dirty air filter.
4. Dirty air stones. Clean with stiff brush under running tap water, or replace stones. Placing stones deeper in tank decreases air flow.

No ↓

1. Check electrical connections.
2. Replace pump.
NOTE: See Aeration under **POWER OUTAGES** in manual.

Is tank water too hot (over 85°)? — Yes → Has water level dropped below the heater's thermostat? — Yes → **Replace evaporated water.**

No ↓   No ↓

1. Improper thermostat setting.
2. Thermostat stuck on.
3. Room temperature too hot.
NOTE: Refer to **WATER CHEMISTRY** for cooling instructions.

If tank water is too cold (under 70°):
1. Improper thermostat setting.
2. Check electrical connections.
3. Broken heating filament.
NOTE: Refer to **WATER CHEMISTRY** for emergency insulating instructions.

NOTE:
For more information on equipment problems, refer to the **EQUIPMENT PROBLEMS** section.

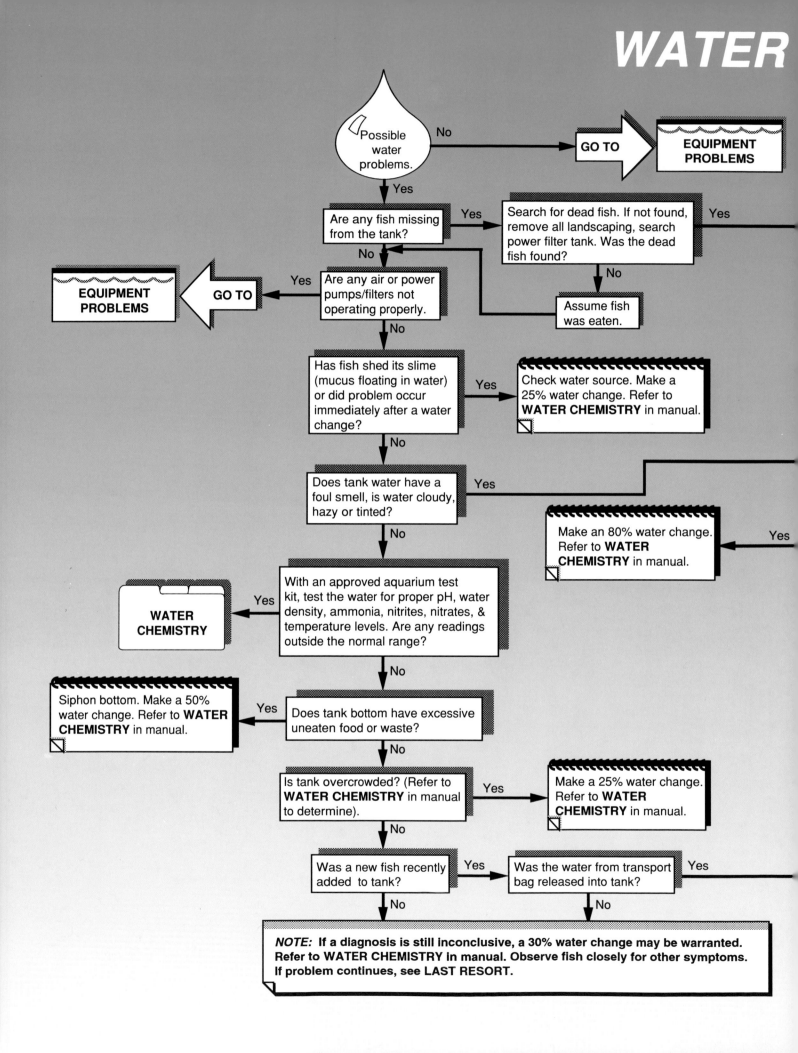

WATER

Possible water problems.

No → GO TO **EQUIPMENT PROBLEMS**

Yes ↓

Are any fish missing from the tank?

Yes → Search for dead fish. If not found, remove all landscaping, search power filter tank. Was the dead fish found?

No ↓

Are any air or power pumps/filters not operating properly.

Yes → GO TO **EQUIPMENT PROBLEMS**

No (from dead fish) → Assume fish was eaten.

No ↓

Has fish shed its slime (mucus floating in water) or did problem occur immediately after a water change?

Yes → Check water source. Make a 25% water change. Refer to **WATER CHEMISTRY** in manual.

No ↓

Does tank water have a foul smell, is water cloudy, hazy or tinted?

Yes → Make an 80% water change. Refer to **WATER CHEMISTRY** in manual.

No ↓

With an approved aquarium test kit, test the water for proper pH, water density, ammonia, nitrites, nitrates, & temperature levels. Are any readings outside the normal range?

Yes → **WATER CHEMISTRY**

No ↓

Does tank bottom have excessive uneaten food or waste?

Yes → Siphon bottom. Make a 50% water change. Refer to **WATER CHEMISTRY** in manual.

No ↓

Is tank overcrowded? (Refer to **WATER CHEMISTRY** in manual to determine).

Yes → Make a 25% water change. Refer to **WATER CHEMISTRY** in manual.

No ↓

Was a new fish recently added to tank?

Yes → Was the water from transport bag released into tank?

Yes →

No ↓ (both)

NOTE: If a diagnosis is still inconclusive, a 30% water change may be warranted. Refer to WATER CHEMISTRY in manual. Observe fish closely for other symptoms. If problem continues, see LAST RESORT.

PROBLEMS

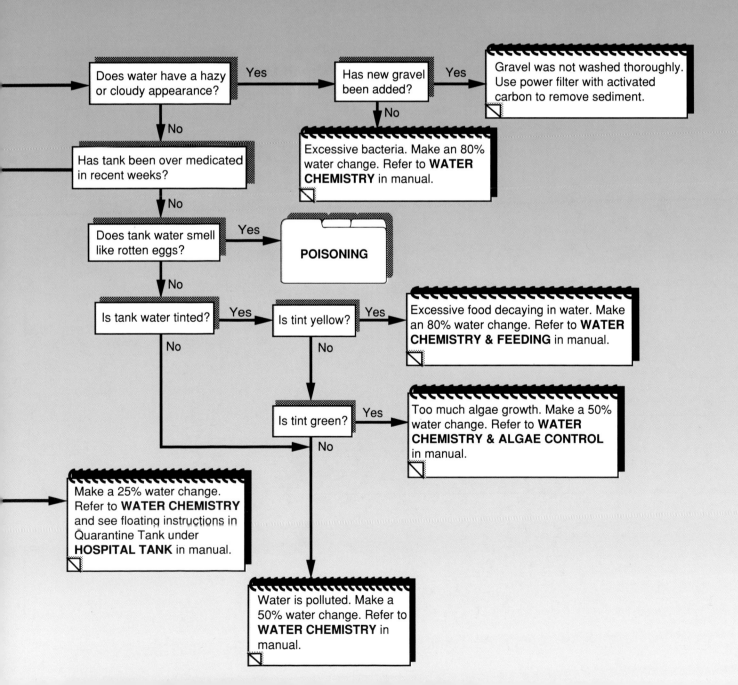

Make a 50% water change. Refer to **WATER CHEMISTRY** in manual.

Does water have a hazy or cloudy appearance?

Yes → Has new gravel been added?

Yes → Gravel was not washed thoroughly. Use power filter with activated carbon to remove sediment.

No

No → Has tank been over medicated in recent weeks?

Excessive bacteria. Make an 80% water change. Refer to **WATER CHEMISTRY** in manual.

No

Does tank water smell like rotten eggs?

Yes → **POISONING**

No

Is tank water tinted?

Yes → Is tint yellow?

Yes → Excessive food decaying in water. Make an 80% water change. Refer to **WATER CHEMISTRY & FEEDING** in manual.

No

No

Is tint green?

Yes → Too much algae growth. Make a 50% water change. Refer to **WATER CHEMISTRY & ALGAE CONTROL** in manual.

No

Make a 25% water change. Refer to **WATER CHEMISTRY** and see floating instructions in Quarantine Tank under **HOSPITAL TANK** in manual.

Water is polluted. Make a 50% water change. Refer to **WATER CHEMISTRY** in manual.

FISH BREATHING PROBLEMS

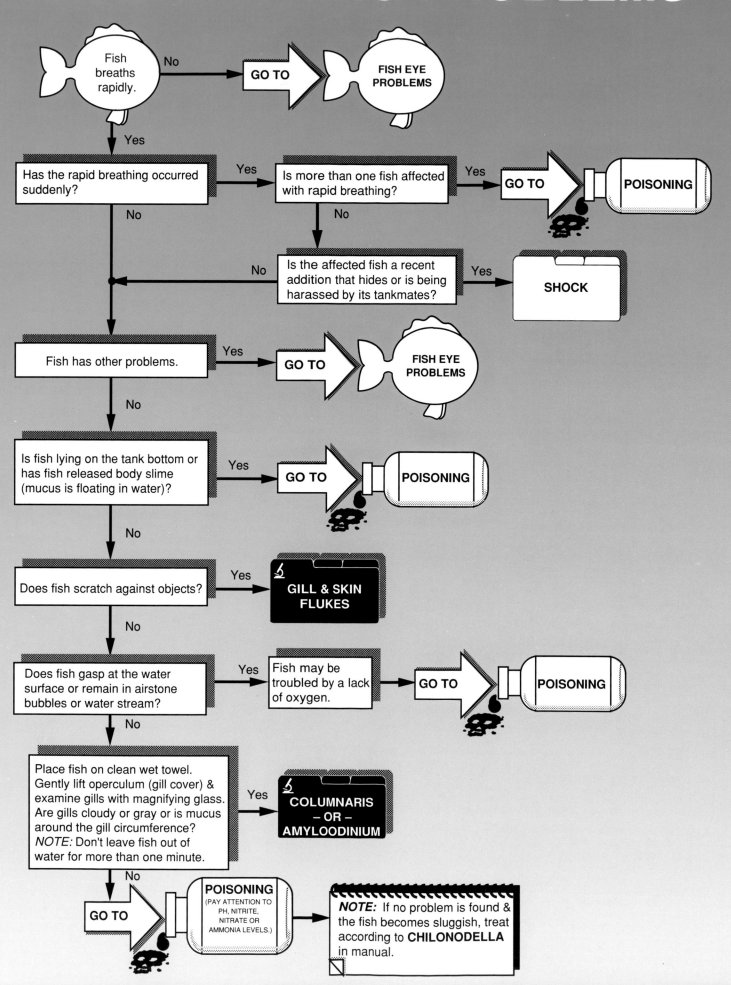

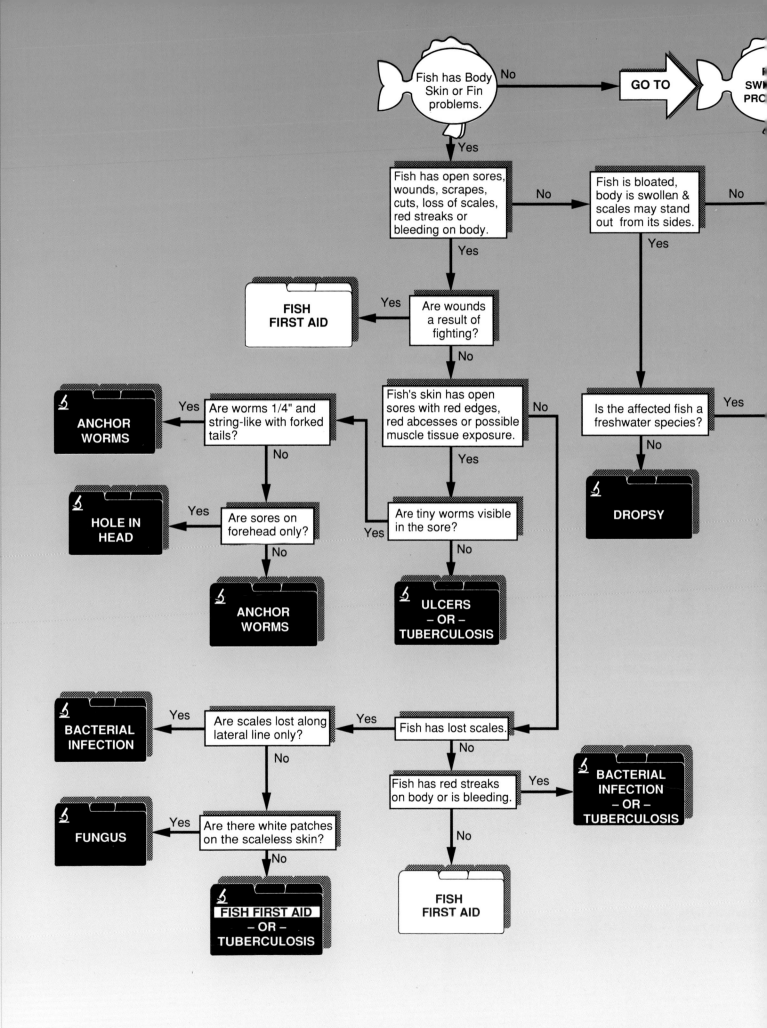

Fish has Body Skin or Fin problems. — No → **GO TO** → SWIM PROBLEMS

Yes ↓

Fish has open sores, wounds, scrapes, cuts, loss of scales, red streaks or bleeding on body. — No → Fish is bloated, body is swollen & scales may stand out from its sides. — No →

Yes ↓ (from open sores)

Are wounds a result of fighting? — Yes → **FISH FIRST AID**

No ↓

Fish's skin has open sores with red edges, red abcesses or possible muscle tissue exposure. — No →

Yes ↓ (bloated) → Is the affected fish a freshwater species? — Yes →

No ↓ → **DROPSY**

Are worms 1/4" and string-like with forked tails? — Yes → **ANCHOR WORMS**

No ↓

Are sores on forehead only? — Yes → **HOLE IN HEAD**

No ↓

ANCHOR WORMS

Fish's skin open sores: Yes ↓

Are tiny worms visible in the sore? — Yes → (to "Are worms 1/4"...")

No ↓

ULCERS – OR – TUBERCULOSIS

(from "No" open sores with red edges) ↓

Fish has lost scales. — Yes → Are scales lost along lateral line only? — Yes → **BACTERIAL INFECTION**

No ↓

Are there white patches on the scaleless skin? — Yes → **FUNGUS**

No ↓

FISH FIRST AID – OR – TUBERCULOSIS

Fish has lost scales: No ↓

Fish has red streaks on body or is bleeding. — Yes → **BACTERIAL INFECTION – OR – TUBERCULOSIS**

No ↓

FISH FIRST AID

FISH
SWIMMING
PROBLEMS

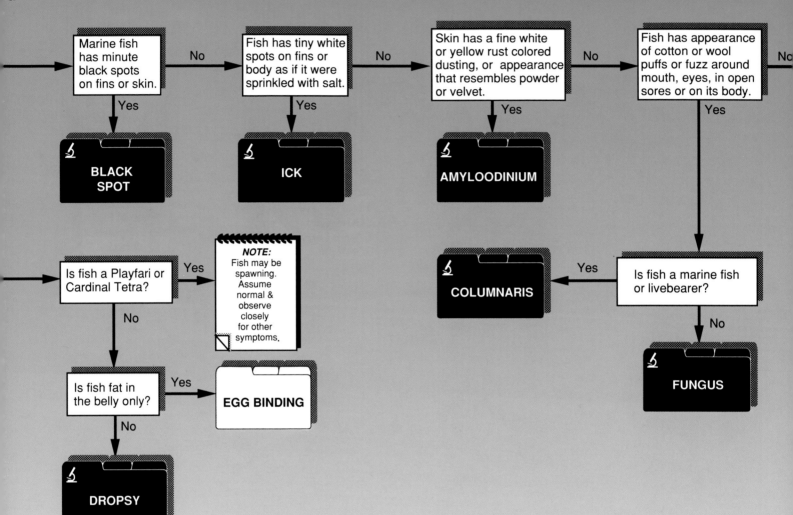

Marine fish has minute black spots on fins or skin.

No →

Fish has tiny white spots on fins or body as if it were sprinkled with salt.

No →

Skin has a fine white or yellow rust colored dusting, or appearance that resembles powder or velvet.

No →

Fish has appearance of cotton or wool puffs or fuzz around mouth, eyes, in open sores or on its body.

No

Yes ↓

BLACK SPOT

Yes ↓

ICK

Yes ↓

AMYLOODINIUM

Yes ↓

Is fish a Playfari or Cardinal Tetra?

Yes →

NOTE: Fish may be spawning. Assume normal & observe closely for other symptoms.

COLUMNARIS

← Yes

Is fish a marine fish or livebearer?

No ↓

Is fish fat in the belly only?

Yes →

EGG BINDING

FUNGUS

No ↓

DROPSY

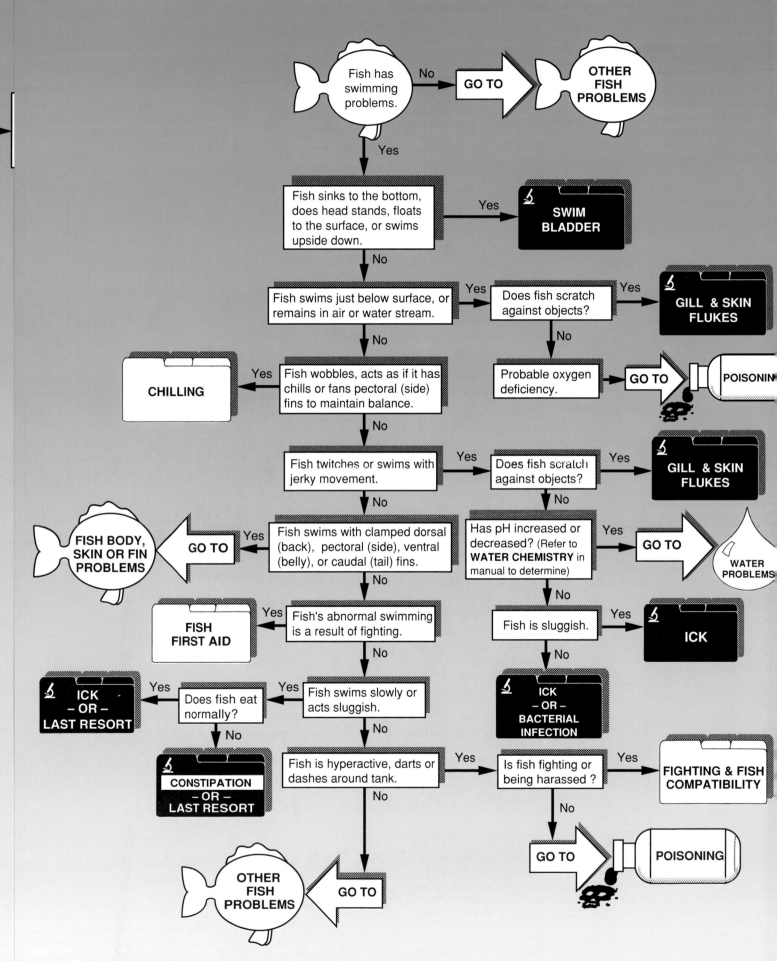

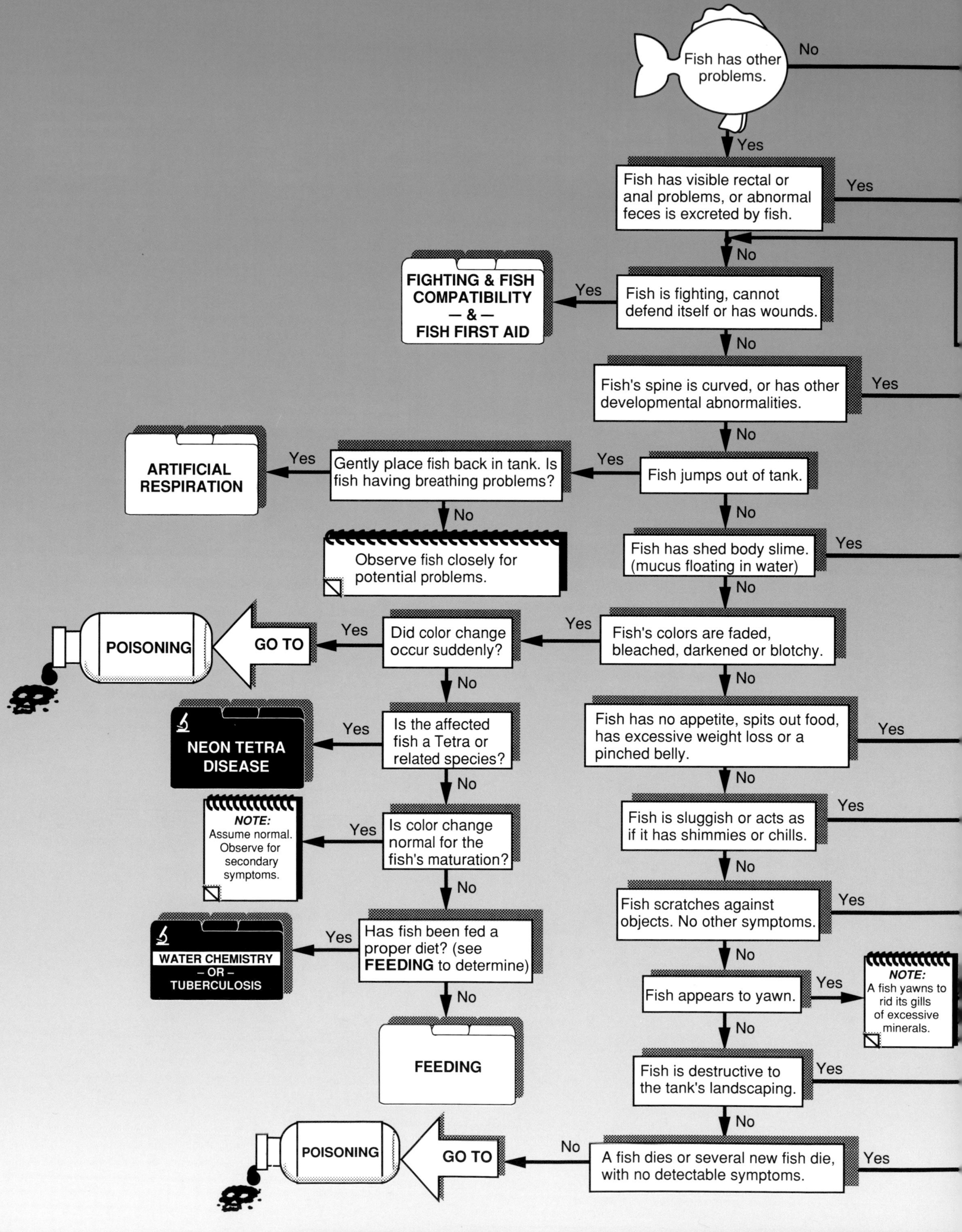

Fish has other problems. — No →

↓ Yes

Fish has visible rectal or anal problems, or abnormal feces is excreted by fish. — Yes →

↓ No

Fish is fighting, cannot defend itself or has wounds. — Yes → **FIGHTING & FISH COMPATIBILITY — & — FISH FIRST AID**

↓ No

Fish's spine is curved, or has other developmental abnormalities. — Yes →

↓ No

Fish jumps out of tank. — Yes → Gently place fish back in tank. Is fish having breathing problems? — Yes → **ARTIFICIAL RESPIRATION**

↓ No (Fish jumps out of tank)
↓ No (breathing problems) → Observe fish closely for potential problems.

Fish has shed body slime. (mucus floating in water) — Yes →

↓ No

Fish's colors are faded, bleached, darkened or blotchy. — Yes → Did color change occur suddenly? — Yes → **POISONING** GO TO

↓ No (colors)
↓ No (Did color change occur suddenly?) → Is the affected fish a Tetra or related species? — Yes → **NEON TETRA DISEASE**

↓ No

Is color change normal for the fish's maturation? — Yes → **NOTE:** Assume normal. Observe for secondary symptoms.

↓ No

Has fish been fed a proper diet? (see **FEEDING** to determine) — Yes → **WATER CHEMISTRY — OR — TUBERCULOSIS**

↓ No

FEEDING

Fish has no appetite, spits out food, has excessive weight loss or a pinched belly. — Yes →

↓ No

Fish is sluggish or acts as if it has shimmies or chills. — Yes →

↓ No

Fish scratches against objects. No other symptoms. — Yes →

↓ No

Fish appears to yawn. — Yes → **NOTE:** A fish yawns to rid its gills of excessive minerals.

↓ No

Fish is destructive to the tank's landscaping. — Yes →

↓ No

A fish dies or several new fish die, with no detectable symptoms. — Yes →

— No → **POISONING** GO TO

PROBLEMS

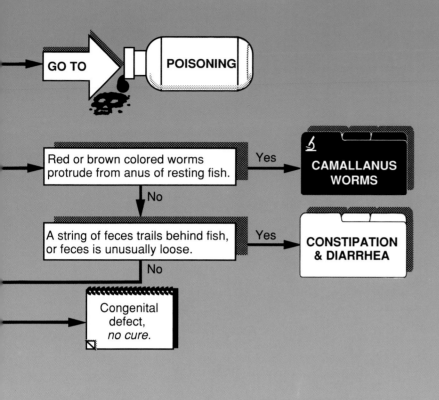

GO TO → **POISONING**

Red or brown colored worms protrude from anus of resting fish. —Yes→ **CAMALLANUS WORMS**

↓ No

A string of feces trails behind fish, or feces is unusually loose. —Yes→ **CONSTIPATION & DIARRHEA**

↓ No

Congenital defect, *no cure.*

GO TO → **POISONING**

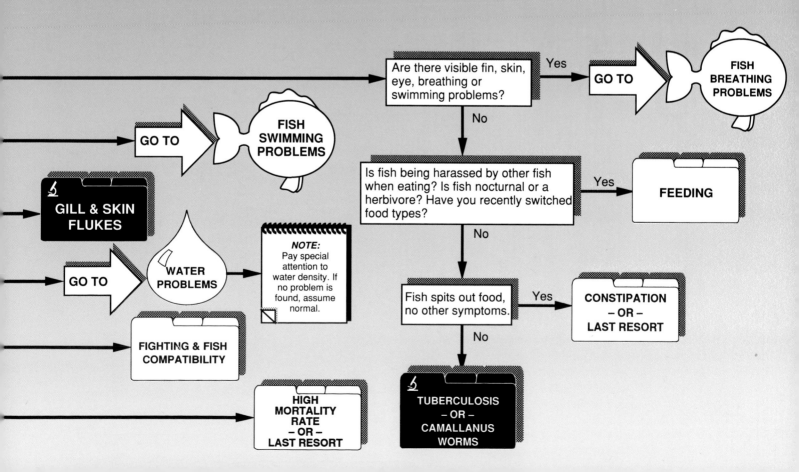

Are there visible fin, skin, eye, breathing or swimming problems? —Yes→ GO TO → **FISH BREATHING PROBLEMS**

↓ No

GO TO → **FISH SWIMMING PROBLEMS**

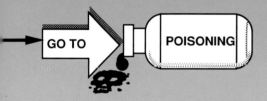
GILL & SKIN FLUKES

Is fish being harassed by other fish when eating? Is fish nocturnal or a herbivore? Have you recently switched food types? —Yes→ **FEEDING**

↓ No

GO TO → **WATER PROBLEMS** →

NOTE: Pay special attention to water density. If no problem is found, assume normal.

FIGHTING & FISH COMPATIBILITY

Fish spits out food, no other symptoms. —Yes→ **CONSTIPATION – OR – LAST RESORT**

↓ No

HIGH MORTALITY RATE – OR – LAST RESORT

TUBERCULOSIS – OR – CAMALLANUS WORMS

POISONING

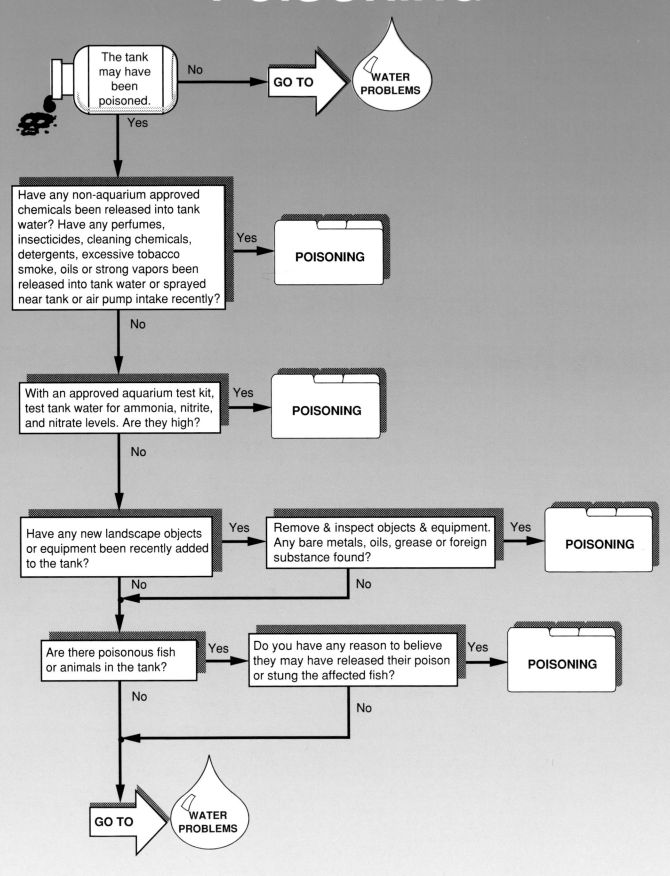

The tank may have been poisoned.

No → GO TO → WATER PROBLEMS

Yes ↓

Have any non-aquarium approved chemicals been released into tank water? Have any perfumes, insecticides, cleaning chemicals, detergents, excessive tobacco smoke, oils or strong vapors been released into tank water or sprayed near tank or air pump intake recently?

Yes → POISONING

No ↓

With an approved aquarium test kit, test tank water for ammonia, nitrite, and nitrate levels. Are they high?

Yes → POISONING

No ↓

Have any new landscape objects or equipment been recently added to the tank?

Yes → Remove & inspect objects & equipment. Any bare metals, oils, grease or foreign substance found?

Yes → POISONING

No ↓

Are there poisonous fish or animals in the tank?

Yes → Do you have any reason to believe they may have released their poison or stung the affected fish?

Yes → POISONING

No ↓

GO TO → WATER PROBLEMS

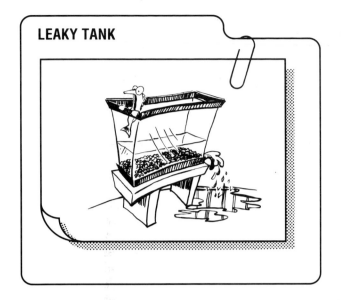

LEAKY TANK

If your tank has any type of leak, take immediate action, or you may have a disaster. If the leak is near the top of the tank, siphon the tank water until the water line is about three inches under the broken seal and refer to **Tank Repair** below.

If the tank has a small leak between the sides of the glass, a temporary seal can be made with two-part epoxy. Mix the epoxy and apply it to the outside of the glass (never on the inside) where the leak is occurring. Note that this is only a temporary solution. The leak still needs to be repaired with proper aquarium sealant.

If the leak is near the bottom of the tank, requiring a complete draining of the tank, siphon the tank water into the hospital tank, buckets, and, if necessary, into one-gallon plastic containers. Save as much of the original tank water as you can by storing it in any container, as long as it is clean and has not been exposed to toxic chemicals. If possible, leave enough water in the tank to keep the gravel wet, so the beneficial bacteria remains alive. You should use one container for each fish. If you run out of containers, use one-gallon plastic water containers with the tops cut off.

Net the fish, place them in the containers and cover with towels. Use a gang valve to divert the air into as many containers as possible. If you have a limited number of airstones, rotate them every hour to the nonaerated water containers. Do not feed the fish during the repair period unless the tank repair takes longer than three days.

If the room temperature is cooler than the desired water temperature, wrap each container with towels and tie with string (see **Water Too Cold** in **WATER CHEMISTRY**). Also, adjust the room thermostat to warm the ambient air enough to keep the water above 72 degrees in the containers.

Tank Repair: If the tank glass has broken, you will need new glass or a new tank. If the seal has broken, scrape the old sealant with a razor blade and thoroughly dry the area to be repaired. Purchase aquarium approved silicone sealant, and follow all manufacturer's instructions. It takes at least two days for silicone to cure.

Replace the tank water with as much of the original tank water as possible, and start all filtration equipment. Replace the floss and carbon in your power filter and drain the water from the filter bowl. Run all filters for two hours before placing the fish in the main tank. Increase aeration to the tank for three days. If you have had to replace the entire tank water, or if the gravel has dried out, the beneficial bacteria may have died, and the tank may have to go through another biological filter cycle (see **POISONING**).

Water Spills: If the water has leaked onto your carpet, blot as much of the water as possible. Place layers of thick towels over the spilled water and apply weight, such as books, or use your feet to help blot the water from the carpet. Don't rub the carpet with the towels, because this may cause the carpet to fray or pill. Remove as much of the water as possible. If you have a wet vacuum, run the vacuum over the area several times after it has been blotted. Place several fans to blow directly on the area. If it is summer and the humidity is high, place a dehumidifier in the room.

If you have spilled a significant amount of water, you may need to rent a large wet vacuum or steam cleaner, and large air moving fans. Never apply soaps or shampoos, since they will leave a residue and will probably stain the carpet.

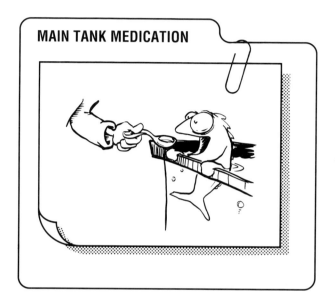

MAIN TANK MEDICATION

Since drugs can upset the biological filter of the aquarium (see **POISONING**), it is highly recommended that you do not medicate the main tank when treating your fish. You should perform all drug therapy in a separate hospital tank (see **HOSPITAL TANK**). However, if treatment must be done in the main tank, follow all pharmaceutical manufacturer's directions for the "net" gallons of your tank. Note that a 50 gallon tank does not hold 50 gallons of water. You must consider the volume of water that has been dispersed by gravel, decorations, animals and equipment; or you will overmedicate the tank.

Before you add medication to the main tank:

1. Remove the carbon from the power filters.

2. Remove all plants, live coral, sponges or invertebrates and place them in a separate hospital tank. Or, you may place them in buckets of siphoned, aerated tank water. Use a gang valve to bleed air to the airstones placed in the buckets. Change the water in the buckets everyday with fresh new water that has been properly prepared and dechlorinated.

3. Increase aeration during the treatment period since some drugs deplete oxygen from the water.

After the treatment period:

1. Return all equipment to normal conditions and perform a 50 percent water change in the main tank.

2. If you have treated the main tank with copper, much of it will have become bound in the bottom gravel or in carbonate base decorations such as tuffa rock or coral. Therefore, gently stir the top layer of gravel and siphon out the debris when making water changes.

3. Replace the carbon and floss in the power filter to help remove the drugs.

4. Keep aeration increased for an additional two days.

5. After one day of running the tank water through the carbon filters, return all plants and aquatic animals to the tank. If they have an adverse reaction to the water, make an immediate 80 percent water change (see **POISONING**).

MERCY KILLING

If you have determined that your fish is suffering greatly and will not live much longer, a humane death may be in order. The most humane method is decapitation.

Small fish can be euthanized without anesthesia. Larger fish should be given an anesthetic first, such as quinaidine sulfate or tricane methanesulfate. These drugs are available from your veterinarian. Prepare a bucket of tank water with 400 mg. of medication for every one gallon of water. Add an airstone and place the fish in the covered bucket for one hour.

Place a wet cloth on a solid surface. Net the fish and place it on the cloth. Hold the fish firmly and make a quick, firm slice with a sharp knife behind the head, severing the vertebrae or head.

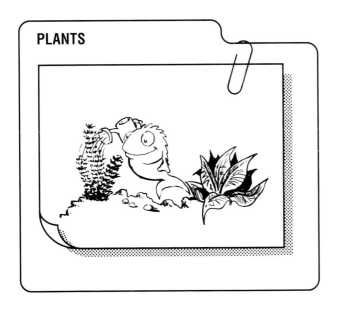

PLANTS

Live aquarium plants need proper care or they can develop problems, and even become diseased. Most live aquarium plant problems are caused by poor water conditions, improper lighting, fish eating or uprooting the plants, improper plant nutrition, or disease. Signs of unhealthy plants include: leaves or stems that become soft, unusually dark or light-colored leaves, unusually thin leaves, mushy or dark-colored roots, or any foul smelling plants.

Symptoms and Diagnosis: In most cases, if an aquarium plant's leaves appear healthy but the roots look unhealthy, the cause is improper water conditions. If the roots look healthy but the leaves appear thin, seem to fray or waste away, the plant probably has a bacterial or fungal disease. Occasional brown leaves are normal, but should be pruned. Numerous brown leaves or abnormally long, thin leaves indicate inadequate aquarium lighting. Abnormally stunted plants or excessive algae growth indicates too much light. Holes in the leaves are usually caused by fish, snails or other aquatic animals eating the leaves.

Water Conditions: An aquarium that is maintained according to the water chemistry section of this manual (see **WATER CHEMISTRY**) should be an ideal environment for most live aquarium plants. Slightly acidic water is generally preferable to hard water because hard water can cause the leaves to turn brown.

Hydroponic plants, are sometimes imported from Europe and are more suited to hard water. To be sure hydroponic plants will tolerate the water in your area, observe the plants in the dealer's tanks for a period of two weeks. If no trouble is noticed, they should tolerate your tank water as well.

Overfeeding plants or fish will cause the tank to become polluted. The excess food floats to the bottom, decays, and the resulting bacteria attacks the roots of the plants. If the leaves appear healthy, but the stem or roots are brown or mushy, the problem is most likely pollution caused by overfeeding.

Many chemicals in the tank water (including chlorine) also cause problems for live plants. Harsh chemicals, such as copper or quinine, should never be used in the presence of live plants. Chemical poisoning usually affects the roots of the plants rather than the leaves. If the plant has been poisoned, you can try to save it by placing it in a bucket of freshly prepared, aerated water for a few hours. There is little chance, however, of saving the plant.

Temperature: Most aquatic plants thrive in water temperatures between 75 to 85 degrees, but if your plants are not from tropical regions, they may require lower temperatures. Swordplants tend to do better in temperatures under 80 degrees. Ask your fish dealer to recommend the proper plant for the water conditions of your community tank.

Planting: One of the most common mistakes aquarists make with live plants is to plant them too deep. The crown of the plant (where the stem and roots merge) should be just above the gravel, not buried beneath it. If the plant tends to become uprooted at this depth, it can be weighted with rocks. Avoid moving the plant around the tank for purely decorative reasons because plants that are constantly being uprooted or transplanted tend to become weak and diseased.

Pruning: Check your aquatic plants daily for any visible problems. Brown, dead, or dying leaves should be pruned. Also prune healthy leaves if the plant is beginning to grow too large.

Fish Uprooting Plants: Large fish may occasionally uproot your plants when digging in the gravel bottom. Moving the plant to the opposite side of the tank, away from the fish's territory, will help avoid this. If the uprooting continues, make sure you have the proper gravel for your plant. If a plant has deep roots, place it deeper, in larger sized gravel. If the plant has small roots, move the plant to the rear of the tank, against the glass. Firmly anchor small rooted plants in the finer-grained gravel, then place a large rock (or rocks) at the base of the plant. Place the rock so the fish cannot gain access to the gravel which holds the plant.

Fish or Animals Eating Plants: Some aquarists purchase plants solely for the purpose of being used as fish food. If this is your choice, purchase less expensive plants, and enjoy watching the herbivores picking at the plants. However, when plants are purchased for decorative reasons, the fish may begin to eat your expensive plants. Most carnivore or omnivore fish, and crustaceans, if kept well fed, will leave the plants alone. Usually, only hungry fish or herbivore fish eat plants. Your fish may especially be prone to eating plants during vacations when no food is given for a few days (refer to **Vacation Feeding** in **FEEDING**). If the animals are well-fed but they continue eating the plants, consider changing the plants or the animals.

Lighting and Feeding: Plants that are abnormally long and thin are reaching for more light, indicating inadequate lighting. Brown leaves or brown algae also indicate insufficient lighting. On the other hand, abnormally stunted plants or excessive algae growth signal too much light. Usually, 12 hours of light each day (a combination of natural and artificial) is sufficient for aquatic plants. Cryptocoryne plants will tolerate low intensity light. Refer to **Lighting** in **WATER CHEMISTRY** for proper lighting requirements. Liquid plant foods and minerals occasionally added to the tank water, help ensure proper plant nutrition.

Delicate Plants: Less hardy aquatic plants include water milfoils, fanworts, or hornworts.

Treatment: Medicating diseased plants is generally not successful. If a plant begins to rot, it is best to simply remove and discard the plant. Otherwise, you may jeopardize the health of your fish community. Since most plant problems are caused by improper water conditions, use the **Water Problems Flow Chart** to correct the water problem before adding another plant.

If your plant roots are mushy, or the leaves are translucent or wasting away, or the roots are rotting or have a foul smell, it is probably from a fungal or bacterial disease. If you want to treat the plant, ask your fish dealer for a broad spectrum bacterial or fungal medication manufactured for aquatic plant root rot. If you cannot find any such medications, purchase an antibiotic manufactured for bacterial infections that contains the drug tetracycline. The plant should be treated in a separate hospital tank, never in the main tank. Refer to **HOSPITAL TANK** for proper setup. Follow all manufacturer's recommendations.

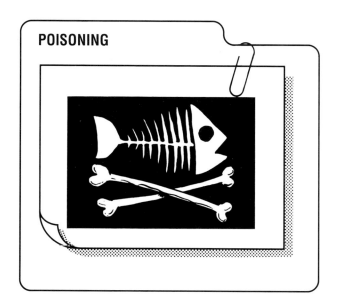

POISONING

Because of the small confines of aquarium life, the slightest amount of toxin can quickly become lethal to fish. If you have determined from the **Poisoning Flow Chart** that your fish are victims of poisoning, you must take corrective action immediately or you risk losing the entire tank of fish!

Toxic Substances: Toxins to aquatic life can take both obvious and concealed forms. If any of the following scenarios have recently occurred in your aquarium, your fish have probably been poisoned: **1)** over medication of main tank (treating multiple diseases within a few weeks time); **2)** chemicals were used around the tank such as perfumes, aerosol cans, excessive tobacco or fireplace smoke, oils, insecticides, cleaning chemicals, paint, detergents that have accidently been placed in the tank or any strong vapors that may have been pumped into the tank by the air pump; **3)** metallic objects have fallen or have been placed in the tank; or **4)** non-approved aquarium sealant was used or sealant was not properly cured.

Other toxic substance poisoning could be a result of heavily chlorinated tap water used in making a water change, improperly sanitized rocks, coral or other decorations, or oil leaking from filtration equipment. In an unsanitary aquarium, rotting debris from the bottom can create hydrogen sulphide poisoning, thus robbing the water of needed oxygen. An indicator of hydrogen sulphide poisoning is that the tank water smells like rotten eggs.

Nitrates, Nitrites, Ammonia and the Biological Filter: The biological filter cycle refers to the process that transforms gravel filter beds in new, unconditioned aquariums into established biological filters. At the beginning of the cycle, fish excretions and uneaten food are trapped in the gravel and begin to decay, forming bacteria and ammonium (ammonia). As the bacteria level rises, it begins to transform ammonium into nitrites (nitrite ions). It is at this stage that ammonium and nitrites can become lethal to the more delicate fish. Eventually, the bacteria transforms the nitrites into less toxic nitrates. Nitrite and ammonium levels will then suddenly drop to near zero and the biological filter cycle is complete.

Fish that are more sensitive to water conditions can now be safely added to the aquarium. The length of time required for the completion of the biological filter cycle depends on such variables as the size of the tank, the quantity of fish, and the amount of oxygen in the water (the more oxygen, the faster the cycle completion). This cycle can range from one week in small aquariums to several weeks in large ones.

An established tank has already completed at least one biological filter cycle. However, excessive medication of the tank or inadequate aeration may have killed enough of the bacteria in the filter bed that your tank may have high ammonia or nitrite levels, or may have started another biological cycle. Medicating diseased fish in a hospital tank only, and maintaining proper water conditions (see **WATER CHEMISTRY**) will virtually eliminate any ammonia, nitrite or nitrate poisoning from occurring in an established aquarium.

Poisonous Fish: Due to the recent interest in keeping more exotic fish in home aquariums, poisonous fish have created a new toxicity problem. Poisonous fish include smooth skinned puffers, boxfish, trunkfish, soapfish, lionfish, scorpionfish, stonefish and stingrays. Other poisonous aquatic animals include anemones, sea apples, sea cucumbers, octopi, cone snails, fire coral, fire sponge, sea urchins, and fireworms.

By their very nature, if poisonous fish become scared or their safety is threatened, they may sting their victim or release their poison, ironically killing some or all of their tankmates, as well as themselves. Poisonous aquatic animals will sometimes release their toxins when diseased or wounded.

If you have the slightest suspicion that poison has been released into the tank water, take immediate corrective steps or you will lose the entire tank of fish! Poison released in the tank by poisonous fish or animals should be treated as any other poisoning. Refer to **FISH FIRST AID** for treatment of fish that have been stung by venomous aquatic fish or animals such as anemones. If the sting is severe, you can expect to lose the fish.

Symptoms: Symptoms exhibited by poisoned fish include sudden darting or wild swimming around the tank, sometimes bumping into objects. Sudden rapid breathing, blotchy coloration, and/or equilibrium problems can occur. You may also see fish suddenly lying on their sides, breathing rapidly.

The key words for a definitive poisoning diagnosis are "sudden" and "most". If rapid breathing occurs "suddenly" and if it is noticed in "most" of your fish, there is some form of toxin in the water.

Some poisoning, such as metallic poisoning, may occur gradually, but most fish that have been poisoned will quickly exhibit symptoms. Therefore, if the symptoms have occurred slowly over several days, your fish is probably not poisoned, but is suffering from poor water conditions or a disease.

Treatment: Immediately remove severely affected fish and place them in a hospital tank filled with freshly prepared water (not from the main tank). See **HOSPITAL TANK** for the proper setup. If it is a marine poisoning, prepare fresh saltwater and add additional water dechlorination buffers (available at your fish dealer) which make the synthetic saltwater safe for immediate use.

If only one or two fish are affected, you can leave the non-affected fish in the main tank. If most of your fish are affected, it is a severe poisoning and you need to remove all of the fish. In this case you may need additional containers, such as plastic buckets, to hold the fish. Be sure that the buckets used have never had cleaning chemicals in them. Provide strong aeration to the containers by branching air from the air pump through gang valves, and attach the air tubing to airstones. Place the airstones in the containers. If a fish is having severe or irregular breathing or is hyperventilating, it may need artificial respiration (see **ARTIFICIAL RESPIRATION**).

As soon as all of the affected fish have been removed, make an immediate 80 percent water change in the main tank. Leave all filtration systems in operation, add activated charcoal to the power filter, and increase aeration by a factor of two.

After one to three hours, fish not severely affected should begin to recover. Continue to monitor these fish for an additional hour. If the fish in the main tank are still not showing symptoms of poisoning, the recovered fish can then be put back into the main tank. Continue treatment of severely affected fish for one day. If it is a severe poisoning, despite all efforts, expect that some fish will die.

After one day, assess the situation. Fish that have now recovered to normal swimming and breathing patterns can now be placed in the main tank. Fish that are recovering but still wobbly should remain in the hospital tank until fully recovered. Siphon as much of the water from the hospital tank as you can into a bucket and replace it with main tank water. If the fish has another adverse reaction to the main tank water, replace the hospital tank water with the water previously siphoned into the bucket. Make a 50 percent water change to the main tank.

Any fish still on their side and breathing heavily are suffering, will not live much longer, and should humanely be put to death. In this case, refer to **MERCY KILLING**.

The key to success in treating poisoning is to take immediate action. Waiting just a few hours can mean the difference between complete recovery and losing the entire stock!

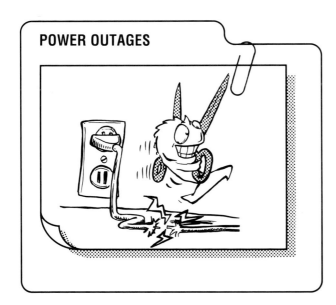

POWER OUTAGES

Occasionally, the power may be lost to your entire system. The severity of this depends on the size, water conditions, and population of your tank, and the duration of the power outage. There are three areas of concern during a power outage: aeration, filtration, and water temperature.

Aeration: As soon as the power filters fail, a rapid buildup of bacteria begins in the tank, causing a loss of oxygen. If the tank is not overcrowded, and you have been maintaining normal water conditions (see **WATER CHEMISTRY** to determine both), there should be enough oxygen to last for six hours before any respiration problems are noticed. If you have a large tank (over 50 gallons), there may be no aeration problems for an even longer period.

Any outages longer than six hours will require some artificial aeration. Find a small plastic or glass pitcher or container. Remove the tank lids, dip the container in the tank, and fill it with tank water. Lift the container about six inches above the water and pour a steady stream back into the tank (watch that you don't splash your walls). When pouring, produce as much surface agitation as possible, which directly causes aeration to the water. Repeat this process for five minutes every hour until the power returns.

If the power is out for several hours, it would be advisable to go to a sporting goods or bait and tackle store and purchase one or two minnow aerators used by fishermen. The aerators are usually powered by a single D cell battery and can give several hours of temporary, emergency aeration. Be sure the aerators are properly rinsed with hot, fresh water before placement in the tank. You may want to purchase an extra aerator to have available as an emergency backup to your air pump.

If the air pump is inoperable, and is located below the water level of the tank, the air tube will act as a siphon and actually draw water into the air pump. This can cause multiple problems, and could ruin the pump. Try to mount your air pump above the water level. If this is not practical, pull the air tubes out of the water when power is lost to the air pump.

Filtration: Any outages longer than two hours can cause the bacteria to reach toxic levels in the cotton floss of the power filter. If the power filter has been inoperative for more than two hours, discard the water and used cotton floss from the filter's container, then replace each with a fresh supply.

Uneaten food quickly decays and pollutes the water, so do not feed your fish until the power has been restored. With a net, carefully remove any excessive fecal waste or food from the gravel bottom.

Water Temperature: During winter months, if the room temperature is less than the tank's water temperature, the tank will begin to cool as soon as power is lost. If the tank is small, the heat from the water will dissipate rapidly. During summer months, if the air conditioning is off, the temperature of the tank water will begin to rise with the room temperature. If the power is off for more than two hours, or you notice a change in temperature of more than five degrees from its normal setting (77 degrees is ideal), you should take action. Refer to **"Water Too Cold"** or **"Water Too Hot"** in **WATER CHEMISTRY** for tank insulating or cooling procedures.

SHOCK

When a fish is frightened, is being harassed by an aggressive fish, is a new addition to the tank, or is having a severe reaction to adverse water conditions, it may suffer a form of shock. Fish can be frightened even by someone turning on the aquarium light in a dark room, or banging on the tank glass. Loud noises and fighting with tankmates also can frighten a fish.

In some cases, the water conditions of your tank may be so different from the fish dealer's tank that a new fish suffers shock when released into your tank. To avoid this, see instructions for floating the transport bag under **Quarantine Tank** in **HOSPITAL TANK**.

Children love to watch the reactions of aquarium fish. Unfortunately, their usual response is to bang on the tank glass. Supervise children when they are around the tank, and teach them proper respect for the animals.

Avoid sudden noises or lighting changes. Place the tank in a room that is not subject to abnormal internal/external environmental noise, such as loud stereos. Turn on a room light for a few minutes before turning on the aquarium light. Likewise, turn off the aquarium light for a few minutes before turning off the room lights.

If more than one fish is affected, or if symptoms of disease are noticed on the fish, the diagnosis of shock should be discounted. Use the flow charts to reach another diagnosis, and treat accordingly.

Symptoms: Symptoms of a fish in shock include: hiding on the tank bottom or in corners or behind objects, clamped fins, blotchy or faded colors, or breathing problems (such as rapid or slow breathing or hyperventilation). Only one fish is affected and no symptoms of disease are visible.

Treatment: The best treatment for shock is to remove the cause. Refer to **WATER CHEMISTRY** to ensure proper water conditions. If the fish is being harassed, refer to **FIGHTING & FISH COMPATIBILITY**.

If the fish has severe breathing problems or is hyperventilating, it may temporarily need artificial respiration (see **ARTIFICIAL RESPIRATION**). If it has been wounded from banging into sharp objects or has been injured by aggressive tankmates, refer to **FISH FIRST AID** for treatment.

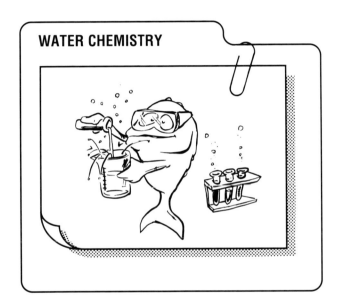

WATER CHEMISTRY

The single most important factor for a successful aquarium is maintaining optimum water conditions. The root of most problems in an aquarium can be traced to some form of improper water condition. In nature, small amounts of pollutants may not always adversely affect the fish because of the vast amount of water in the fish's habitat. However, because of the small water quantities available to aquarium life, even a seemingly insignificant change in water conditions can affect an entire tank of fish within a few days.

Improperly maintained aquariums are a breeding ground for multiple diseases. Once a disease is established it can reach epidemic proportions within a few days. If you want to minimize your risk of nearly all aquarium problems and achieve a successful, healthy, and thriving aquarium, the secret is this: **"MAINTAIN PROPER WATER CHEMISTRY!"**

At the end of this section is a summary of proper water maintenance. Use this summary as a guide to achieve optimum water conditions.

Factors for Proper Water Chemistry: Many aquarists believe that maintaining proper water conditions refers only to timely water changes. However, to ensure optimum water chemistry you also need to monitor such factors as temperature, pH, nitrites, nitrates, ammonia, water density, aeration, pollution, lighting, feeding, and overcrowding. Equipment must also be properly maintained.

Water Changes: Routine water changes are the most important part of water chemistry maintenance. Generally, a 25 percent water change should be made every two to three weeks. Use a bucket with gallon graduations to make the water removal and refilling process consistent.

Before making water changes, be sure that all the utensils to be used are thoroughly cleaned and rinsed with hot, fresh water only (not with soap). Water treatments should be used to remove chlorine from the tap water. Stir the top layer of the gravel with the siphon to remove excessive debris. The replacement water should have relatively the same temperature and water density as the main tank.

Once the water has been replaced, make sure all filtration equipment is operating properly. Inspect all equipment and replace the cotton filters in the air and water pumps. Increase aeration for at least one day after making a water change.

Temperature: Although fish come from all of the oceans, most thrive in aquarium water with a temperature between 73 to 83 degrees. The ideal water temperature for most marine and freshwater fish is 77 degrees. If you have cold water fish, you may need to keep the temperature significantly colder. Therefore, you cannot keep these fish with tropicals. If you are unsure, consult your fish dealer for the water temperature requirements of your specific species.

Water temperature problems are usually caused by a faulty heater. Refer to the **Equipment Problems Flow Chart** for proper diagnosis. Other heating problems can be caused from room temperatures or tank locations.

Water Too Hot: The tank should not receive direct sunlight or be placed over a heat register. If the tank water becomes dangerously hot (over 85 degrees) from summer room temperatures or heater problems, quick action should be taken to cool the tank.

To cool the tank water, close the blinds or curtains in the tank room or place brown paper or cardbord around the tank to deflect sunlight. Unplug the tank heater and turn off the lights on the tank, as well as any incandescent lights in the room. Place ice cubes in plastic bags and float the bags in the tank. Plastic (not metal) containers filled with water and then frozen can be floated in the tank or placed in the power filter box.

It is important to decrease the tank temperature slowly, by no more than one degree every five hours, to its normal range. Higher temperature water contains less oxygen, so you will need to increase aeration until the water temperature returns to normal.

Water Too Cold: If the tank water has become too cold (under 70 degrees), quick action should be taken to retain the heat before it dissipates. Close the windows or turn off any fans or air conditioners that are producing cold drafts around the tank. If it is winter, turn the heat up in the room, or use a space heater a few feet away from the tank.

If the water temperature is below 68 degrees, wrap the tank sides in layers of blankets (not electric blankets) and tie with a rope. Plastic containers, such as water jugs, can be rinsed and filled with hot (not boiling) water, then capped tightly and placed in the tank. Place a thick blanket over the tank lid(s).

Depending on the size of the tank, you now have about 24 hours to repair or replace the tank heater or fix any other source of the problem. Once the heating problem has been corrected, adjust the heater's thermostat to slowly increase the temperature to the normal range by one degree every five hours.

Pollution: Overfeeding or untimely water changes are the primary causes of water pollution. Foul smelling, cloudy or tinted water, debris on the tank bottom, or a rotting, dead fish are all indications of polluted water. If the water has become polluted, perform a 50 percent water change. Then, if still polluted, perform another 50 percent water change. Increase aeration for one day whenever you perform a water change.

Overcrowding: A tank with too many fish cause unnecessary territorial fights, excessive fecal waste, and rapid oxygen or trace element depletion. You may be wondering then, how many fish are too many? It depends on the type of fish, and the size and shape of the tank. Every fish should be given a safe place to hide, enough room to swim, and enough water to derive sufficient oxygen. If any of these conditions are not met, your tank is overcrowded.

The proper level of oxygen is a primary factor in determining overcrowded conditions. The majority of oxygen is absorbed into the water at the surface, not from the air bubbles. Therefore, the amount of fish you may safely keep is directly proportional to the surface area of your tank.

For all traditional shaped tanks, a rule of thumb for freshwater fish is one inch of fish for every net gallon of water. The marine rule is one inch of fish for every three net gallons of water. For small odd shaped tanks, it doesn't matter that you have a ten-gallon tank if the water surface area is the same as a traditional style five-gallon tank. This tank can hold no more fish than the five-gallon tank could. This is not necessarily so in larger odd shaped tanks if you have high powered aeration and filtration equipment.

Water Density: Water density (specific gravity) is the measurement of the amount of salinity in water; therefore, water density is generally not a concern in a freshwater aquarium. Density levels are measured with the use of a hydrometer, available at your fish dealer. Marine aquariums require that specially prepared mixes be combined with fresh water to produce synthetic seawater.

The proper range for saltwater density is a specific gravity reading of 1.020 to 1.024 with an ideal reading of 1.022 at 80 degrees Fahrenheit. High levels of salinity can cause an excessive buildup of salt on the fish's gills, causing respiratory problems. Low levels of salinity can cause equilibrium problems for fish.

Incorrect density levels usually occur from improper saltwater preparation or evaporation. Unusually high density levels can be corrected by the addition of fresh water to the tank. Low levels can be corrected with the addition of the saltwater mix.

Aeration: Not only is aeration necessary for fish life, but it is also essential for any other plants or animals you may have in the tank. Although most oxygen enters the water from the surface (surface agitation is greatly encouraged), aeration is still necessary within the aquarium. The deeper the tank, the more a powerful pump is needed. Follow your fish dealer's recommendation to properly size the air pump to your tank.

Over time, you may find that the air flow may be decreasing. This can be caused from constricted air hoses (even within the pump), faulty gang valves, dirty air filters, faulty diaphragms, dirty airstones, or a faulty pump. Airstones can be cleaned with a stiff brush, under running, fresh water. If, after cleaning the airstones, the air flows freely for a few days and then a noticeable constriction of air occurs, replace the airstones. Never place the air pump near strong fumes or open chemicals. Always increase aeration when making a water change or when the tank water temperature is over 80 degrees.

Place the air pump above the water level of the tank, if possible. If the pump fails and has been placed below the water level, the air tube acts as a siphon and draws tank water into the pump. This can cause multiple problems, if not destroy the pump.

pH: The pH test determines whether your tank water is too acidic or too alkaline. Acceptable freshwater pH ranges are 6.8 to 7.3 with an ideal reading of 7.0. Proper marine pH ranges are 8.0 to 8.5 and the ideal is 8.4.

The fastest way to correct an improper pH reading is to perform a water change, but the cause of the improper pH reading must also be found. Excessively high pH levels are considered alkaline and can cause the fins of freshwater fish to fray (confusing the diagnosis of fin or tail rot), or their color to pale. Low pH levels indicate acidic water and can cause complications such as rapid breathing in fish. A severe drop in pH can cause death relatively quickly. If the pH is low, it could indicate polluted water or a tank overcrowded with fish or plants. Most incorrect pH levels are caused by improper water conditions. Use the **Poisoning** and **Water Problems Flow Charts** to find the cause of the improper pH reading.

If the pH is incorrect, a 30 percent water change should be made. Run all filtration equipment for two days and then check the pH again. If the pH is still incorrect, pH buffers and alkaline treatments, available at your fish dealer, should be added.

Water Hardness: Usually, water hardness is not a problem for established aquariums. If you suddenly suspect a water condition problem but have not changed your water source, you can rule out water hardness. If you have a new aquarium and live in an area with unusually hard water, have your fish dealer test a sample of tap water for water hardness. If there is a slight problem, the dealer will have water conditioning buffers available to solve the problem.

If hardness is a major problem, you will probably need a water softener for household use, thus alleviating the aquarium water hardness problem. In most cases, soft water is fine for general aquarium use. However, soft water can cause complications for some fish during breeding and water softeners can also cause a buildup of salt in the tank water, affecting water density. If you are using a water softener, monitor water density levels.

Lighting: The tank should receive at least 12 hours of light a day. Indirect sunlight can be used during the day, while the use of a fluorescent aquarium strip light can be used during the evening. Avoid incandescent lighting, since the bulbs can contribute to overheating the aquarium during hot summer months.

Algal growth is also an essential part of healthy water chemistry. Algae needs light to grow. The key to knowing if the proper amount of light is being used, is to observe the color and amount of the algae. Brown algae indicates insufficient lighting. Green algae indicates proper lighting. Excessive algal growth indicates too much lighting (see **ALGAE CONTROL**).

Nitrates, Nitrites, Ammonia and the Biological Filter: Refer to **POISONING**.

Summary of Proper Aquarium Maintenance: While you are giving the daily visual check to all of your fish, also give your tank and equipment a visual exam. Look for properly operating filtration equipment, and proper air flow. Check the color, smell and temperature of the water. Scrape excessive algae growth. Check live plants for dead leaves. Net any uneaten food as well as excessive debris or fecal matter, and check the breathing rates of all the fish.

Perform a 25 percent water change every two to three weeks with water that has the same temperature and density as the tank water. Increase aeration for one day after every water change. Keep all equipment properly maintained, and replace the cotton filters in the air and water pumps when you make water changes. If you follow these rules, you should eliminate most potential aquarium problems!

FISH DISEASES

AMYLOODINIUM

This protozoan disease is similar to Ick, and care should be taken by the aquarist not to confuse the two during diagnosis (see **ICK**). Ick usually takes the form of small individual pinhead sized, white spots on the fish's tail, fins or body and looks as if someone had sprinkled salt on the fish. Amyloodinium (commonly known as Oodinium or Velvet) usually looks like someone had dusted the fish with a fine whitish gray (on marine fish) or yellowish rust (on freshwater fish) colored powder. This causes the fish to have a "velvet" appearance, hence the name. However, Dwarf Ick (or Invisible Ick) reproduces at one-third to one-half of the adult size and can be easily confused with Amyloodinium. Therefore, if the fish has the dusty appearance but does not respond to the Amyloodinium treatment, treat the fish for Ick.

Amyloodinium can also attack the fish's gills and have no visible body symptoms except a small amount of extra mucus on the gills. The mucus usually can only be seen when the operculum (gill cover) is lifted for examination.

As with most diseases, Amyloodinium is able to infect the fish when the fish's resistance has been weakened by shock, sudden temperature changes, improper water conditions, overcrowding or an improper diet. A fish that has recently been added to the tank can also be a carrier of Amyloodinium. Therefore, like most diseases, the best way to prevent Amyloodinium from occurring is to maintain optimum water conditions (see **WATER CHEMISTRY**), provide a proper diet (see **FEEDING**), and allow a two week quarantine for new additions before placing them in the main tank (see **Quarantine Tank** in **HOSPITAL TANK**).

Amyloodinium has a life cycle of five to eight days. At this stage, the parasite reproduces by cell division. The new juveniles number from 100 to 1000 and then free-swim in search of a new host. It is during this period that the proper medication can kill the juveniles before they find and infect a new host. In other Amyloodinium infestations, the disease may be covered by fish mucus or skin and thus will repopulate on the same host fish.

Symptoms: The fish's skin has a whitish gray or yellowish rust colored, velvety appearance. The fish usually exhibits rapid breathing and may swim directly in the water stream or air stream. The fish may also scratch against the tank bottom, have dull eyes and exhibit loss of appetite.

Treatment: The most effective treatment for Amyloodinium is copper sulfate. Since copper can be moderately harmful to the beneficial bacteria in the gravel bottom, treatment should be given in a separate hospital tank. See **HOSPITAL TANK** for proper setup. If you must medicate the fish in the main tank, refer to **MAIN TANK MEDICATION**.

Since Amyloodinium can be fatal rapidly, quickly prepare and medicate the hospital tank with the proper "Oodinium" (marine) or "Velvet" (freshwater) medicine available at your fish dealer. If you have a marine aquarium, the best cure for Amyloodinium is copper sulfate. If you have a freshwater aquarium and do not want to use copper, there are non-copper medications packaged for velvet that contain such drugs as quinine sulfate, quinine hydrochloride, chloroquine phosphate, or acriflavine. Ask your fish dealer to recommend the brand that has been the most successful.

Net and quickly place the infected fish in the hospital tank. If more than one fish shows the Amyloodinium symptoms, quarantine and treat those fish as well. Lights will diminish the strength of quinine and other such drugs, so turn off any lights on the hospital tank and keep the tank as dark as possible. Increase aeration to ease breathing problems, and slowly (by one degree every five hours) increase the temperature to about 85 degrees. Maintain these conditions throughout a two week treatment period.

After the treatment period, keep the recovered fish in the hospital tank for one additional week to be sure a relapse does not occur. Decrease the water temperature by one degree every five hours until it matches the temperature of the main tank. If the fish has recovered after the additional week, return the fish to the main tank. Observe all fish closely for a second outbreak of the disease. If the fish has partially recovered but remains sluggish and sickly, it may be infected by a bacterial disease. If this is the case, or if the treatment was unsuccessful, treat the fish according to **BACTERIAL INFECTION.**

⬛ ANCHOR WORMS

Anchor worms are small parasitic crustaceans that may attach themselves to a freshwater fish's body. The worms appear as a 1/4-to 3/8-inch piece of string that has a forked tail. Anchor worms that grow large are easily detectable and cause considerable distress to the host fish. In most cases, the parasite is introduced into the aquarium from live foods. Anchor worms also bore through the skin of the fish, creating ulcerations or blood spots on the fish's body. Don't confuse this ulceration with those caused by bacterial diseases (see **ULCERS**). The difference is that the parasites are not visible in the open sore with bacterial disease.

Symptoms: Clear to white or brown string-like worms, with forked tails are visible on the skin, head or mouth of the fish. Open sores may appear on the fish's skin with the worms protruding from the sore.

Treatment: If the worms are large, it is best to remove the worms rather than medicate the fish. Net the fish and place it on a clean, wet towel. With a pair of tweezers, carefully pull each worm from the fish "with the grain". Dip a cotton swab in a broad spectrum antiseptic such as betadine (available at drug stores). Dab the swab on the wound where the worm was attached. Let the drug penetrate for ten seconds, then place the fish directly back in the main tank. Do not keep the fish out of the water for more than one minute.

If the worms are very small, like fine threads, it is best to medicate the fish. Ask your fish dealer for an anti-parasitic medication manufactured for use against Anchorworms or Fish Lice such as trichlorfon. Treat the fish in the hospital tank (see **HOSPITAL TANK** for proper setup) and follow all pharmaceutical manufacturer's recommendations.

Note: If you must medicate the fish in the main tank, refer to **MAIN TANK MEDICATION**.

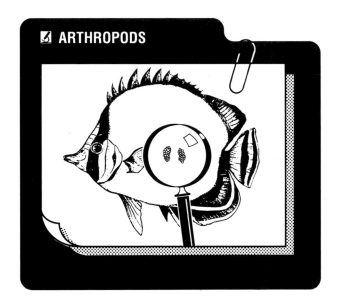

Occasionally, fish that are new additions to the aquarium will be carriers of parasitic worms and crustaceans. If the fish has what appears to be tiny eggs attached to a worm on the fish's gills or body, it is most likely an Arthropod. The parasites are more easily seen under a magnifying glass.

Symptoms: Tiny clusters of round nodules (eggs) are attached to a small wormlike parasite on the fish's skin, gills, or eyes. In some cases, only the eggs can be seen.

Treatment: Use medications manufactured for use against **ANCHOR WORMS**. Treat the fish in a separate hospital tank. See **HOSPITAL TANK** for proper setup.

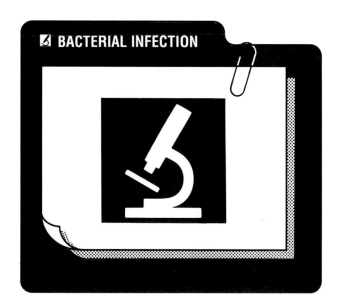

There are several bacterial diseases that can infect aquarium fish. Many times the symptoms of bacterial disease can be visible on the fish. Such common diseases include Fin Rot, Ulcers and Dropsy. Other bacterial infections are virtually impossible to differentiate without performing several laboratory tests. It is not necessary, however, that you identify the specific bacterium before you can treat the fish.

Bacterial diseases are usually present in unsanitary tanks. Therefore, to help prevent the disease, maintain proper water conditions (see **WATER CHEMISTRY**).

Symptoms: Cloudy eyes, open sores (ulcers) on the body or lateral line, abscesses, rotting or inflammation (reddening) of the skin, fins or internal organs, bulging eyes or rapid breathing are all possible symptoms of a bacterial disease.

Treatment: A fish infected with a bacterial disease should be treated in a separate hospital tank. See **HOSPITAL TANK** for proper setup. The best medication is a broad spectrum gram negative antibiotic such as nitrofuran (furan) or kanamycin sulfate. There are other packaged antibiotic medications for bacterial diseases such as aureomycin, neomycin sulfate, tetracycline, oxytetracycline, nitrofurazone, or nalidixic acid. If you can't find a medication that contains furan or kanamycin sulfate, ask your fish dealer to recommend the brand that has been the most successful. Follow all manufacturer's directions.

It is important to treat the fish at the full recommended dosage as well as for the entire treatment period in order to prevent a second occurrence of the disease. If you have an ultraviolet light, it should be left on in the main tank to help control the spread of the disease.

Note: If you must medicate the fish in the main tank, refer to **MAIN TANK MEDICATION**.

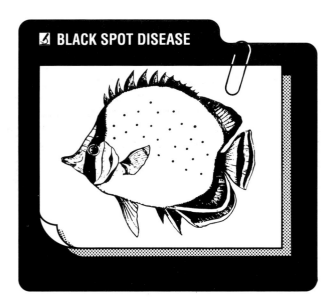

Black spot disease is a generic term for minute, black, parasitic flatworms that attach themselves to the skin and internal organs of marine fish. The worms usually enter the aquarium from a recent addition to the tank. If left untreated, death is probable. Yellow tangs seem to be especially susceptible to this parasite.

Symptoms: Tiny black specks appear on a marine fish's tail, fins, or body.

Treatment: There are several medications that are specifically manufactured for black spot disease. Ask your fish dealer to recommend the most successful medication and follow all manufacturer's recommendations. It is best to treat the fish in a separate hospital tank. See **HOSPITAL TANK** for proper setup.

Note: If you must medicate the fish in the main tank, refer to **MAIN TANK MEDICATION**.

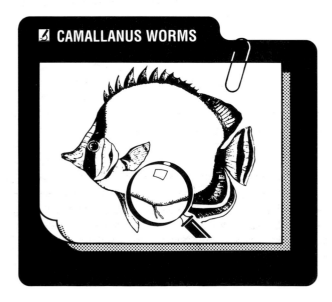

Camallanus are small red or brown worms that attach themselves to the rectum and intestines of the fish. If Camallanus worms are present, the rectum usually becomes enlarged and inflamed. The worms can actually be visible protruding from the anus of a resting fish. When the fish swims, however, the worms withdraw inside the intestine.

Symptoms: A resting fish may have red or brown worms protruding from its anus. The fish may also appear pinched in the belly.

Treatment: Ask your fish dealer to recommend a proper (marine or freshwater) medication for internal parasitic worms. Most medications for internal worms include such drugs as trichlorfon, yomesan or piperazine. Follow all manufacturer's recommendations and treat the fish in a separate hospital tank. See **HOSPITAL TANK** for proper setup.

Your fish dealer may also have prepackaged, medicated food that should be fed to the affected fish during the treatment period. If the food is unavailable, add 50 mg. of piperazine, available from a veterinarian, to ten grams of the fish's food. Feed the piperazine medicated food every other day for one week.

Note: At no time should you try to pull the worms from the fish. The worms have a firm bite, and would rip the lining of the fish's intestines if pulled from the fish. If you must medicate the fish in the main tank, refer to **MAIN TANK MEDICATION**.

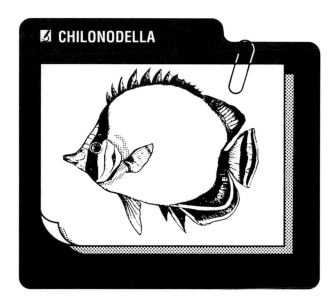

Chilonodella is a parasitic disease that attacks the skin and gills of the fish. The usual result is an excessive secretion of mucus on the body, which causes the skin coloration to appear dull, cloudy or hazy. Chilonodella infections create a large buildup of mucus on the gills, causing severe breathing problems. Usually, the cause of Chilonodella is improper water conditions or improper nutrition. Refer to **WATER CHEMISTRY** and **FEEDING** for prevention.

Symptoms: The fish has excessive mucus on its body or gills, as well as cloudy or hazy skin and colors. Rapid breathing and sluggishness are also symptoms. In some cases, only rapid breathing is noticed, followed by lethargy and eventual death.

Treatment: Treat the same as for **ICK**. If this treatment is not successful for a marine fish, give it a formalin bath as described in **GILL & SKIN FLUKES**.

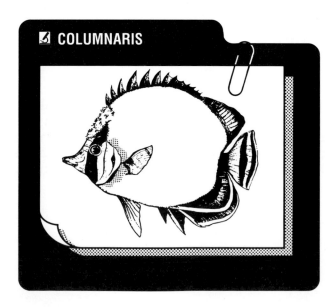

This bacterial disease is often confused with fungus since both diseases have similar symptoms (see **FUNGUS**). Most freshwater "fungal" symptoms are true fungus infections. Nearly all marine fish and some freshwater livebearers' "fungal" symptoms are actually bacterial in origin. Many times the bacterium is columnaris. Therefore, a rule of thumb for fungal symptoms is to treat freshwater fish according to **FUNGUS**, and marine and livebearer fish according to **BACTERIAL INFECTION**.

The fuzzy puffs of columnaris, usually around the gills, mouth, or in open sores and wounds are actually strings of bacteria, not fungus.

The best way to diagnose columnaris is to net the fish and place it on a clean, wet towel. Gently lift the fish's operculum (gill cover) with a tongue depressor and examine the gill filaments under a magnifying glass. If you spot erosion at the tip of the gill filaments, the fish most likely has columnaris. Do not keep the fish out of the water for more than one minute.

Columnaris is found in tanks that have poor water quality. Therefore, to prevent columnaris, maintain proper water conditions (see **WATER CHEMISTRY**).

Symptoms: Close examination of gills reveal erosion at the filament tips. The affected fish has mucus or small string-like puffs on its gills, opercula, mouth or skin, and may exhibit rapid breathing.

Treatment: Same as **BACTERIAL INFECTION**.

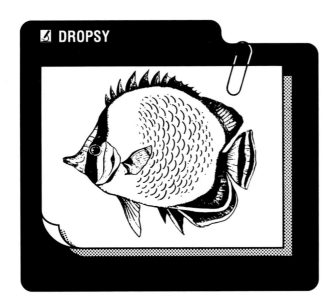

Dropsy is a bacterial disease that attacks nearly all the internal organs of the fish, causing a concentration of fluids in body tissues or cavities. This results in a general swelling of the fish's abdomen, thus causing the scales to protrude from its body.

Be careful when making the diagnosis not to confuse dropsy with egg binding (see **EGG BINDING**), natural spawning cycles, or just an obese fish. The scales of a male Cardinal Tetra or Playfairi will stand out from his body during spawning periods. This is normal, but would give a false symptom of dropsy. Tuberculosis can also cause the body to swell and the scales to protrude. However, treatment for dropsy is virtually the same as for Tuberculosis.

Symptoms: The body will have general swelling with protrusion of scales. The eyes may also bulge.

Treatment: Dropsy is not very infectious. However, the treatment for its bacterial cause requires that the fish be treated in a separate hospital tank. See **HOSPITAL TANK** for proper setup.

Medicate the hospital tank with a proper (marine or freshwater) antibiotic manufactured for dropsy or gram negative bacterial infections, such as nitrofuran (furan) or kanamycin sulfate. These medications are available from your fish dealer. If you can't find a furan drug or kanamycin, there are other packaged antibiotic medications that contain such drugs as aureomycin, neomycin sulfate, tetracycline, oxytetracycline, or nalidixic acid. Ask your fish dealer to recommend the brand that has been the most successful. Follow all manufacturer's recommended instructions.

Maintain the same tank temperature as your main tank (77 degrees is ideal). If you have an ultraviolet light, it should be left on in the main tank to help control the spread of the disease.

Note: If you must medicate the fish in the main tank, refer to **MAIN TANK MEDICATION.**

It should be noted that dropsy is not an easy disease to cure. If the fish is severely infected, or if you have exhausted attempts for recovery, you may need to consider a painless and instant death for your fish. If this is the case, refer to **MERCY KILLING.**

Fins that are badly frayed or disintegrating for reasons other than fighting, usually indicate fin or tail rot. Fin or tail rot is a bacterial disease that usually attacks weak or slightly damaged fin edges. Once established, the bacterium slowly consumes the fin as it works its way toward the body. This causes the fins to appear frayed, ragged or, in severe cases, nearly stubs.

Frayed fins can also be a result of tank water that is high in pH. Therefore, before you treat for fin rot, be sure that the water conditions have been ideal. The best prevention for fin or tail rot is to maintain proper water conditions (see **WATER CHEMISTRY**) and keep fish from fighting or nipping their tankmates' fins (see **FIGHTING & FISH COMPATIBILITY**).

<u>Symptoms:</u> The fish's tail or fins are frayed or ragged, and may appear to be decaying or shrinking. Goldfish and other long-tailed fish may have red streaks in their veiltails.

<u>Treatment:</u> Since fin rot is a bacterial disease, it is best treated with antibiotics. There are many different medications for fin rot available from several pharmaceutical manufacturers. Have your fish dealer recommend the most successful marine or freshwater antibiotic medicine that is specifically manufactured for fin or tail rot.

Treat the fish in a separate hospital tank. See **HOSPITAL TANK** for proper setup. Follow all of the manufacturer's directions for medication. If you have an ultraviolet light, it should be left on in the main tank to help control the spread of the disease.

In some cases, a secondary infection of fungus is present. If this is the case, treat the fish for fin rot first, then treat for fungus (see **FUNGUS**). If you must medicate the fish in the main tank, refer to **MAIN TANK MEDICATION.**

FUNGUS

In most cases, fungus (Saprolegina) is a secondary infection. If a fish has an open wound caused from injuries or even a recent disease which penetrated the skin, the lack of mucus covering would leave the wound area temporarily unprotected. During this period, the wound could be susceptible to a secondary infection from fungus.

To prevent fungus: avoid overcrowding, remove sharp objects from the tank, use a fine mesh net or glass jar when transferring fish, do not suddenly frighten fish, ensure fish compatibility (see **FIGHTING & FISH COMPATIBILITY**) and maintain optimum water conditions (see **WATER CHEMISTRY**).

Most freshwater "fungal" symptoms are true fungus infections. Nearly all marine fish and some freshwater livebearers' "fungal" symptoms are actually bacterial in origin. Many times the bacterium is columnaris (see **COLUMNARIS**). Therefore, a rule of thumb for fungal symptoms is to treat freshwater fish according to **FUNGUS**, and treat marine fish and livebearers according to **BACTERIAL INFECTION**.

Symptoms: The fish has patches of white or gray cottony, fuzzy puffs attached to its skin, fins or in wounds. The fish's eyes may also be cloudy or have a film covering them. There may also be excessive mucus production on the fish's gills, or around the circumference of wounds. Fungus is usually a freshwater fish infection.

Treatment: If medicated quickly, fungus is usually easy to cure. There are several packaged fungicide medications available. Most include such drugs as acriflavine, neutroflavine or copper sulfate. Have your fish dealer recommend the brand that has been most successful, and follow the manufacturer's instructions.

Fungal medication is sometimes applied directly on the patch of fungus with a cotton swab. If the pharmaceutical manufacturer recommends direct application of the medicine, net the fish and place it on a clean, wet towel. Dip a cotton swab in the medication and then dab the swab directly on the fungus. Do not keep the fish out of the water for more than one minute. Quickly place the fish in a hospital tank (see **HOSPITAL TANK** for proper setup). Since fungus is usually a secondary infection, use the **Fish Problems Flow Charts** to then determine the primary infection, and treat the fish accordingly. If the primary cause cannot be determined, treat the fish in the hospital tank with a broad spectrum antibiotic, according to **BACTERIAL INFECTION**.

Note: If you must medicate the fish in the main tank, refer to **MAIN TANK MEDICATION**.

GILL & SKIN FLUKES

Gill and skin flukes are microscopic worm-like parasites that attach themselves to the gills or body of the fish. Even under 10x magnification, only the largest flukes can be seen. The tiny transparent worms are extremely distressful to fish, causing them to swim wildly and scratch their body or opercula (gill coverings) on the tank bottom or sharp objects. The worms tend to spread quite rapidly, covering most of the gills, causing considerable damage and leaving the fish susceptible to lethal bacterial infections.

<u>Symptoms:</u> The fish scratches against the gravel or tank decorations, has clamped fins, exhibits rapid breathing, may swim wildly or near the water surface. The fish's gills may have excessive mucus or turn a dull gray. Livebearers show signs of clamped dorsal or anal fins and become lethargic.

<u>Treatment:</u> Gill flukes can be successfully treated with formalin baths or with medication in a separate hospital tank.

If a formalin bath is the desired treatment, and the fish is not too large, place the fish in a three-gallon bucket of siphoned, aerated tank water. Medicate the bucket of water with 600 mg. of formalin to every one gallon of water. Place an airstone in the bucket, cover the bucket and leave the fish in the bath for 30 minutes. If at any time, the fish becomes listless, exhausted or loses its equilibrium, immediately place it back in the main tank. If the fish then experiences severe or irregular breathing, or is hyperventilating, it may need artificial respiration (see **ARTIFICIAL RESPIRATION**).

If you want to treat the fish with specific gill fluke medication, see **HOSPITAL TANK** first for the proper setup. There are several medications specifically manufactured for treating gill flukes. The most common packaged anti-fluke medications include such drugs as formaldehyde or trichlorfon. Ask your fish dealer to recommend the most successful marine or freshwater medicine for gill flukes. Follow all manufacturer's directions.

Note: If you must medicate the fish in the main tank, refer to **MAIN TANK MEDICATION**.

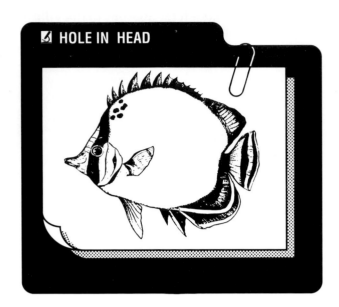

This is a generic name for the parasitic disease Hexamita, and it is primarily introduced into the tank from live foods such as feeder fish and tubifex worms. Poor water conditions or poor nutrition can contribute to the spread of the disease. The disease is more prominent in Cichlids, Discus and Catfish and can be both internal and external. If external, the disease becomes evident by small visible round holes in the head area.

To help prevent Hexamita, ensure proper water chemistry (see **WATER CHEMISTRY**), proper nutrition (see **FEEDING**) and restrict the use of live foods.

Symptoms: Fish has tiny, round holes in the head area. Close examination usually reveals small, whitish strings (worms) inside the hole.

Treatment: Net fish and treat it in a separate hospital tank. See **HOSPITAL TANK** for proper setup. Ask your fish dealer to recommend a proper (marine or freshwater) medicine for Hole in the Head disease. Note that medications may not be specifically manufactured for Hole in the Head. Instead, the disease may be listed on labels of medicine for cures of other diseases. If none is found, use drugs manufactured for the treatment of flagellates such as metronidazole. Follow all manufacturer's instructions.

In addition, increase the amount of roughage in the diet by feeding more algae, lettuce and green vegetables (see Omnivores in **FEEDING**). You will need patience; this is a difficult disease to cure.

Note: If you must medicate the fish in the main tank, refer to **MAIN TANK MEDICATION**.

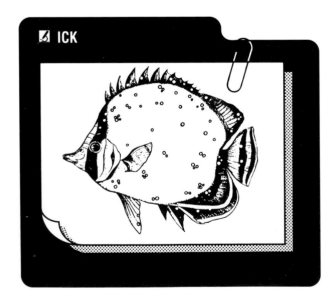

Ick (or Ich) is probably the most common parasitic disease among tropical fish. Freshwater Ick (Ichthyophthirius), or marine Ick (Cryptocaryon) is almost always present in an aquarium and infects fish that are in poor health or have had a recent infection that has temporarily left them without certain immunities. Ick can soon become visible on a fish if the fish's natural resistance is weakened from shock, unsuitable water conditions, overcrowding or an improper diet. A fish that has been recently added to the tank can also be a carrier of Ick. Therefore, like most fish diseases, the best way to prevent Ick from occurring is to maintain optimum water conditions (see **WATER CHEMISTRY**), provide a proper diet (see **FEEDING**), and allow a two week quarantine for new additions before placing them in the main tank (see Quarantine Tank in **HOSPITAL TANK**).

The life cycle of Ick is usually three to five days, during which time it releases itself from the fish and floats to the bottom. At this stage, the parasite reproduces by cell division. The new juveniles number from 100 to 1000 and then free-swim in search of a new host. It is during this period that the proper medication can kill the juveniles before they find and infect a new host. In other Ick infestations, the disease may be covered by fish mucus or skin, and thus, will repopulate on the same host fish.

If treatment begins as soon as the symptoms are first noticed, your fish can usually be cured of Ick. The key to controlling and curing fish of Ick is to quarantine the fish before the juvenile spores are released into the main tank. If left untreated, however, Ick can kill a fish within a few days. After a few life cycles, Ick may become so rampant that it may kill all the fish in the tank!

Symptoms: A fish that has contracted Ick will generally have a few small white dots on the fins or body. As the disease spreads, the fish will have the appearance that it has been sprinkled with salt. Other symptoms of Ick may include the fish scratching against the gravel, rapid breathing, cloudy eyes, cloudy fins and/or some fin deterioration.

Don't confuse Ick with Amyloodinium (see **AMYLOODINIUM**). Ick usually has distinct, individual pinhead sized white dots. Amyloodinium's spots are smaller and clustered closer together, which gives the dusty or "velvet" appearance. However, Dwarf Ick (or Invisible Ick) reproduces at one-third to one-half of the adult size and can be easily confused with Amyloodinium.

Treatment: At the first signs of Ick, the fish should be treated in a separate hospital tank. Refer to **HOSPITAL TANK** for proper setup. Medicate the hospital tank with a proper marine or freshwater Ick (or Ich) medicine available at your fish dealer. The most common external parasitic control drugs packaged for use against Ick are malachite green, aureomycin, benzaldehyde, quinine hydrochloride, or quinine sulfate. Ask your fish dealer to recommend the brand that has been the most successful. Follow all manufacturer's instructions. Turn off all the aquarium lights and keep the hospital tank as dark as possible. Increase aeration to ease breathing problems, and increase temperature slowly to about 85 degrees, at a rate of one degree every five hours. Maintain these conditions throughout the treatment period (at least ten days).

Note: If you must medicate the fish in the main tank, refer to **MAIN TANK MEDICATION**.

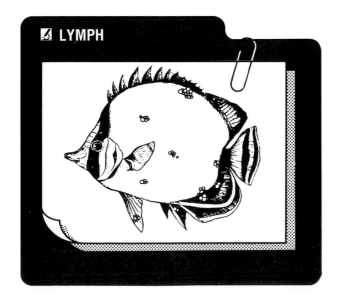

Lymphocystis is a viral growth that can appear on the fins and skin of aquarium fish. Lymph can be distinguished from other tumors by its distinctive appearance. Close inspection of the Lymphocystis nodule reveals white to gray cauliflower or raspberry-like growths that usually begin at the tips of the fish's fins and may eventually spread to other areas of the fish's body. Usually, the cause of Lymph is from unusual stress, such as shock (see **SHOCK**). Lymph that appears on new additions to the tank is most likely caused from the stress of capture and transport.

Symptoms: White to gray, cauliflower or raspberry-like growths on the fins or body of the fish.

Treatment: Since lymph is not very contagious or fatal, the best treatment is to leave the fish in the main tank and let the disease run its course. If you have an ultraviolet light, keep it on to stop the spread of the virus.

If the Lymph tumor covers most of the mouth, causing eating problems for the fish, the growth should be removed. If you want to perform the surgery, net the fish and place it on a clean, wet towel. With a scalpel or new razor blade, carefully trim the portion of Lymph that is obstructing the mouth. Be careful not to cut into the actual skin, if at all possible. Disinfect the area by dabbing it with a cotton swab dipped in a broad spectrum antiseptic such as betadine (available at drug stores). Let the drug penetrate for ten seconds then place the fish directly back in the main tank. Don't keep the fish out of the water for more than one minute. If you do not want to perform the surgery yourself, contact a veterinarian.

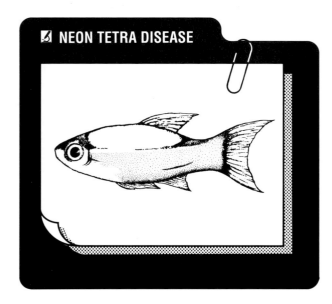

NEON TETRA DISEASE

This is the parasitic disease, Plistophora, most common among neon tetras and related species. The disease usually enters the fish by way of infected food. Diseased fish appear pale, and tetras eventually lose their red stripe. The whitish area of the skin is actually deteriorating muscle tissue. Note that fading can also be caused from improper water conditions. Therefore, before treating for neon tetra disease, be sure that your water conditions have been ideal (see **WATER CHEMISTRY**).

Symptoms: The fish has pale colors and loses its red stripe. The fish may also have swimming problems, and exhibit some weight loss.

Treatment: There are several medications available for neon tetra disease. Unfortunately, these medications have had limited success against Plistophora. Ask your fish dealer for a recommendation of the most successful neon tetra disease medication, and follow all manufacturer's recommendations. Treat the fish in a separate hospital tank. Refer to **HOSPITAL TANK** for proper setup.

Note: If you must medicate the fish in the main tank, refer to **MAIN TANK MEDICATION**.

Popeye is a generic term for Exophthalmos, and refers to a condition that causes the eye of the fish to abnormally bulge from its socket. Popeye can be caused from bacterial diseases, abscesses and tumors, eye injuries, as well as over-aerated water. If left untreated, the eye may bulge so far from its socket that it pops out, resulting in the loss of the eye. If the fish has other signs of disease, use the **Fish Problems Flow Charts** to determine the cause and treat accordingly.

Symptoms: One or both eyes protrude from the socket(s). Some fish also exhibit a lack of appetite.

Treatment: First, eliminate the possibility of over-aeration. If you have been using high-powered power heads that shoot streams of air into the tank water, your fish may be a victim of nitrogen supersaturation. The tiny air bubbles enter the fish's bloodstream and can accumulate behind the eye, causing it to protrude.

The treatment for nitrogen supersaturation, is to turn the power head water stream adjustment to its lowest setting. Temporarily shut the air off to the power heads, and allow the air pump to be the only source of air. Observe the popeye for a few days. If nitrogen supersaturation was the problem, the eye should begin to recede. If no improvement is noticed, or if it worsens, assume the problem is bacterial in nature. Follow the treatment recommended for **BACTERIAL INFECTION**.

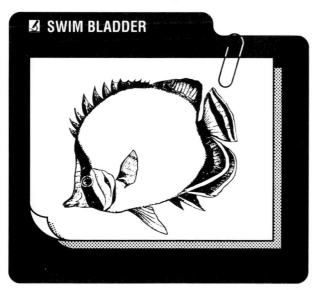

Swim (or air) bladder problems occasionally occur in aquarium fish. When the bladder is affected, the fish experiences equilibrium problems. Sometimes, the problem is not the bladder itself but other problems which indirectly affect the bladder. Diseased and inflamed internal organs, improper water conditions or nutrition, and wounds received from fighting can also affect the equilibrium of the fish.

The key to a swim bladder diagnosis is that no other symptoms of disease are visible and water conditions have been ideal. If there are signs of disease, use the **Fish Problems Flow Charts** to determine the cause and treat the fish accordingly.

Symptoms: The fish has buoyancy problems. The fish may float to the surface, sink to the bottom, swim with its head down or do headstands on the gravel. At the later stages of the disease, the fish may lose its balance or even swim upside down.

Treatment: There is no specific medical treatment for swim or air bladder disorders. If the origin of the problem is not from a disease, the fish may recover on its own. Since environmental conditions can affect the equilibrium of the fish, pay special attention to the density and temperature of the tank water (see **WATER CHEMISTRY**) and ensure that the fish has had proper nutrition (see **FEEDING**).

If any other symptoms are visible, use the **Fish Problems Flow Charts** to determine a diagnosis and treat the fish accordingly. If the water conditions and feeding are normal, and no other symptoms are noticed, assume the cause is from a bacterial infection. Treat according to **BACTERIAL INFECTION**. Note that if the fish floats or swims upside down, the disease is severe and recovery is not likely.

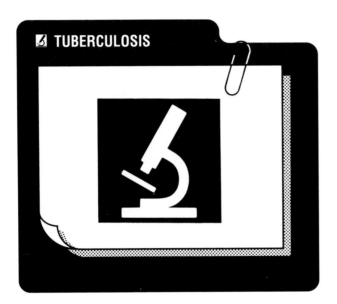

Tuberculosis refers to Mycobacteria that attacks various internal organs of the fish. Since tuberculosis has symptoms similar to other major diseases, it cannot be positively diagnosed without a postmortem. Although attributable to several causes, tuberculosis is generally associated with poor water conditions (see **WATER CHEMISTRY**) or poor nutrition (see **FEEDING**).

Mycobacteria is quite contagious to fish that are of the same species as the infected fish and it can also spread to tankmates of other species as well. Care should be taken if you suspect tuberculosis, since there is a slight chance of human infection from the tubercular fish. Rubber gloves should be worn whenever you place your hands in the aquarium or work with potentially infected utensils.

Symptoms: Pale colors, bulging eyes, rapid breathing at the surface, sluggish movements, hiding, swelling of the abdomen (causing raised scales), no appetite and pinched belly or a wasting away of the fish are all possible symptoms of tuberculosis.

Treatment: Since tuberculosis is infectious, the affected fish should be treated in a separate hospital tank. Refer to the **HOSPITAL TANK** section for proper setup. If you must medicate the fish in the main tank, refer to **MAIN TANK MEDICATION**.

Tuberculosis is difficult to cure. Since it is a very slow growing bacterial disease, the best medication is a broad spectrum gram negative antibiotic such as nitrofuran (furan) or kanamycin sulfate. Other packaged antibiotic medications include such drugs as aureomycin, neomycin sulfate, tetracycline, oxytetracycline, nitrofurazone, or nalidixic acid. If you can't find one that contains furan or kanamycin sulfate, ask your fish dealer to recommend the brand that has been the most successful. Follow all manufacturer's dosage recommendations. Continue the treatment for two to four weeks. If, after the treatment period, the fish is eating and acting normally, you can return it to the main tank. If you have an ultraviolet light, make sure it is on in the main tank to help prevent the spread of the disease to other tankmates.

It should be noted that tuberculosis is not only infectious, but can be a difficult, if not impossible, disease to cure. It may be best to sacrifice the fish for the benefit of its tankmates. If a painless and instant death is required, refer to **MERCY KILLING**.

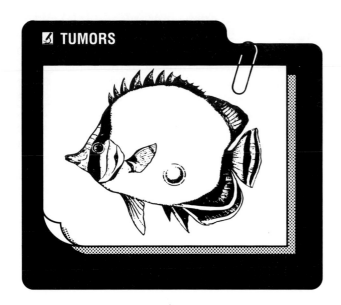

TUMORS

Occasionally, internal and external tumors become apparent among aquarium fish. Although unpleasant to look at, many tumors are benign, and fish seem unaffected by them and can live a normal life. However, others may be cancerous and will continue to grow to enormous sizes, causing distress and eventually death to the fish.

A viral tumor known as Lymphocystis (see **LYMPH**), will usually rectify itself if left alone. Most other tumors, however, need specialized attention that only a fish veterinarian can provide.

Symptoms: Lumps or growths appear on or beneath the skin of the fish. If the growth is underneath the operculum (gill cover), it is probably a swollen thyroid. If the lumps are white to gray raspberry-shaped nodules on the fins or skin, see **LYMPH**.

Treatment: If the tumor is small, does not affect the fish, is not unpleasant to look at and is not growing at a rapid rate, it can be left alone. There is no need to isolate the fish, since tumors are usually not infectious.

As with humans, thyroid tumors in fish can be caused from a lack of iodine in the diet. If the tumor is under the gill of the fish causing the operculum (gill cover) to remain open, the problem is most likely a swollen thyroid and the fish can be treated with potassium iodide. Place the fish in a separate hospital tank. See **HOSPITAL TANK** for proper setup. Add one milligram of potassium iodide (available at drug stores) for every gallon of water. Redose proportionally after every water change. The treatment period can take up to four weeks.

Surgery performed by the hobbyist is not a practical option for a fish tumor. Tumors are well supplied by blood, and after removal, the wound area would need to be cauterized. Large tumor removal would require suturing, which rarely holds on a fish's skin.

If the tumor is causing obvious distress or problems for the fish, a humane death may be in order. If this is the case, refer to **MERCY KILLING**.

ULCERS

Ulcers refer to open sores (ulcerations) on the fish's body. Ulcers usually are caused from the bacterium Vibrio that forms a lump on the fish's skin and eventually hemorrhages. The ulceration gives the appearance of one or more round eruptions of the skin, with red abscesses or red edges around the ulcer. In some cases, the ulcer can become quite large and expose muscle tissue. Don't confuse this disease with sores caused from anchor worms (see **ANCHOR WORMS**). The main difference is that the ulcers do not have visible parasites in the open sores.

Bacterial diseases are usually caused from improper water conditions or improper nutrition. Refer to **WATER CHEMISTRY** and **FEEDING** for prevention of bacterial diseases.

Symptoms: The fish has one or more open sores on its body or the base of its fins, and the sore has red edges or a red abscess. The fish may also have red fin edges or fin rot (see **FIN or TAIL ROT**), lack of appetite, or exhibit sluggish behavior.

Treatment: Treat the same as **BACTERIAL INFECTION**. If treatment is unsuccessful, and the affected fish is a marine fish, the protozoan disease Uronema may be the cause. In this case, treat the fish according to **ICK**.

Fish Disease Photos

Amyloodinium

Amyloodinium

*Bacterial Infection
(superficial)*

Chilodonella
(slime disease)

Columnaris
(mouth fungus)

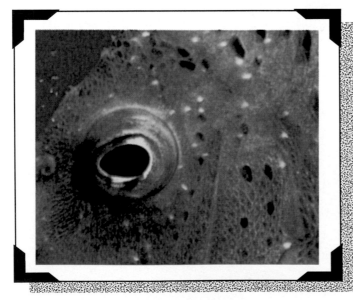

Cryptocaryon
(marine ick)

Dropsy

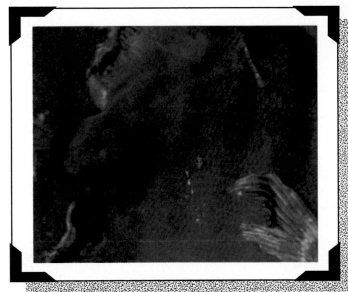

*Fin Rot
(bacteria)*

*Fungus
(saprolegnia)*

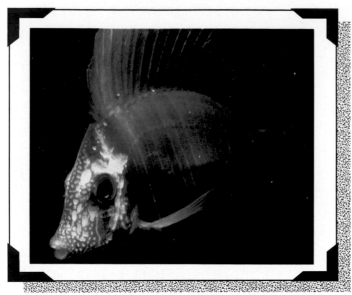

Hole in Head
(symptons similar for
Lateral Line disease)

Ick

Popeye

EQUIPMENT PROBLEMS

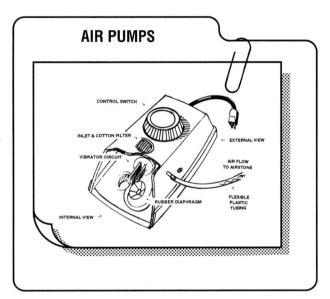

AIR PUMPS

CONTROL SWITCH

INLET & COTTON FILTER

VIBRATOR CIRCUIT

RUBBER DIAPHRAGM

INTERNAL VIEW

EXTERNAL VIEW

AIR FLOW
TO AIRSTONE

FLEXIBLE
PLASTIC
TUBING

The air pump provides critical aeration for the aquarium by pumping bubbles of air into the tank. The bubbles eventually rise to the water's surface helping circulate the water and exchanging carbon dioxide for essential oxygen. The pump incorporates an AC transformer, coil and magnet type of circuit to create a simple vibrator. Attached to the arms of the vibrator is a rubber diaphragm. When the circuit is engaged, the vibrating diaphragm acts as a pump to draw air into the intake, pass it through a filter and out through flexible plastic tubing to the airstones in the aquarium.

Air Pump Tips

Get a large size air pump with an adjustable flow control (you won't be sorry even if you have a small tank). If possible, don't place an air pump below the water level of the aquarium. If the power or pump fails, the plastic tubing will act as a siphon and draw water from the tank into the air pump. This will most likely damage the air pump. Replace the air filter whenever you change the filter medium in the water filter. Methodically maintain (clean and lube if needed) the pump as described in the instruction manual.

Air Pump Problems

Always remember to disconnect all electrical devices from the power source before you begin any repair.

Loud Clattering Sound - This sound is made when the diaphragm has slipped or becomes ruptured. Examine the diaphragm for signs of damage. Slip the diaphragm back on the vibrator arm or replace it if damaged. If it slips off again, it has stretched and must be replaced.

Air Flow has Decreased - This can be caused by a number of problems. First, be sure you haven't bumped the air flow control (if the pump has one). Next, check for clogged airstones, or an air leak or clogging somewhere down line such as outlet tubes, gang valves, bleed valves, or plastic flexible tubing (even inside the pump). Also look for pin holes, loose fitting or crimped plastic tubing or even a very dirty air filter.

Airstones are a common cause of decreased air flow. A quick test is to pull them off the air pump and listen if the air pump is working significantly easier. The flow of air through the stone can be helped by scrubbing it under hot water with a small brush. This usually is a temporary fix. If it works for a few days and then the air flow decreases again, purchase new stones. Note that placing the stones deeper in the tank will increase the resistive water pressure to the pump causing a decrease in air flow (see Aeration in **WATER CHEMISTRY**).

If the problem is somewhere else down the air line, disconnect the pump from the down line tubing. Now reconnect the tubing network one piece at a time. Start at the branch closest to the pump and move toward the end, until you find where the leak or clog is occurring.

Pump is Dead - If the pump makes no noise, you have an electrical problem and it is most likely the transformer. Check your plugs, switch, and electrical connections carefully before you discard the pump.

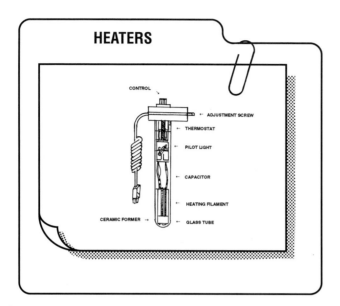

There are many types of heaters available for aquariums. Some are self contained and fully submersible, some are positioned inside a mat on the aquarium bottom and others are attached to the outside of the aquarium glass with suction cups. The most popular aquarium heater is the glass tube heater/thermostat combination that sits on top of the aquarium and extends into the water.

The glass tube aquarium heater consists of a heating coil element (usually nichrome wire) wrapped around a ceramic inner core insulator called a former. The heater is controlled by a simple thermostat consisting of two metal strips that have different expansion rates when exposed to different temperatures. A plastic screw is provided to adjust the distance between the two metals, which in turn leaves the heater turned on for either more or less time. This entire unit is housed within a glass tube and sealed at the top with a plastic, silicone or rubber stopper.

Heater Tips
If possible, place heaters next to tank currents such as water inlets/outlets. This will help disperse the heat throughout the tank. Never bury a heater in the gravel or behind decorations (unless it is a mat heater specifically made for gravel). You may want to purchase two heaters to use one as a backup. Keep the tank water at the proper level for the heater's thermostat. Watch that a fish doesn't become stuck behind the heater and get burned. If the aquarium water becomes too hot or cold, refer to Water Too Hot or Water Too Cold under **WATER CHEMISTRY**.

Heater Problems
Always remember to disconnect all electrical devices from the power source before you begin any repair.

Thermostat Stuck "On" - If the neon pilot light stays on continuously, either the room is quite cold, the water level is below the heater's thermostat, or the bimetal wires of the thermostat are stuck together. If the problem is the water level, either raise the water level or if possible, lower the heater farther into the tank. If the wires are stuck together, repair as described in Dirty Thermostat Contacts below.

Broken Filament - Occasionally, the filament wire breaks. This is usually caused by excessive heating of the coil or an accidental bumping of the heater by the aquarist while the wire is hot. If the wire breaks, you will need to replace the wire. A temporary repair can usually be made by twisting the broken filament wires together with needle nose pliers. This type of repair usually works for just a few days. At your first opportunity, either replace the filament or purchase a new heater.

Cracked Glass Tube - Glass usually cracks from the heater being turned on outside of the tank and then being placed in the water. To avoid this, always unplug the heater before removing it from the aquarium or when you make water changes. If the glass breaks, it can be temporarily repaired with silicone sealant. However, you will still need a new glass tube (see Shock below).

Shock - If you feel a tingling on your hand when it is placed in the water there is probably some type of electrical leak in the aquarium. When the glass tube breaks on the heater, the aquarist will most likely feel the electricity (especially marine aquarists because of the electrical conductivity of salt water). Always unplug a broken heater before touching it or reaching your hand in the water.

Dirty Thermostat Contacts - If a heater has been used for a considerable length of time, the bimetal contacts may become corroded and either not make contact or stick together. In either case, they can be cleaned with sandpaper. If the contacts are stuck together, carefully pry them apart with a small screwdriver. Be careful not to bend the metal pieces or you will severely uncalibrate your heater's thermostat. Gently rub the contact points with fine grit sandpaper until the corrosion is removed. Clean the contacts with tuner wash spray (the nonlubricating kind used on dirty television controls) or use a cotton swab dipped in cleaning alcohol (the type used to clean cassette tape heads).

Blown Fuse - In some heaters, a small wire may be used as a fuse. If an electrical problem occurs with the heater, or if it overheats, the fuse may blow. Replace the fuse with the proper type of wire fuse (never bypass a fuse). If it blows again, the heater has an electrical problem and you should either trouble-shoot it or purchase a new heater.

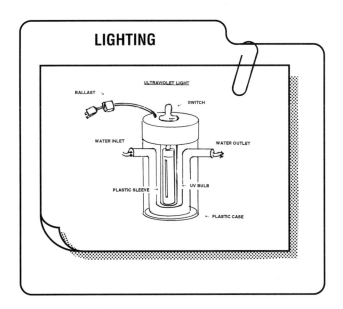

Lighting is an essential part of an aquarium's ecological and biological balance. Aquarium lighting is provided by both natural (sun) and artificial sources. For more information on proper lighting, refer to Lighting under **WATER CHEMISTRY**.

Strip Lighting
Most aquariums today derive their artificial light from long fluorescent bulbs encased in a plastic strip reflector hood that sits on top of the aquarium. The entire circuitry includes electrical wire, a switch, ballast, starter and bulb.

Ultraviolet Lights
Ultraviolet lights are used by some aquarists to help control the spread of disease in the aquarium. UV lights are usually connected to the outlet of the water filter where water passes through the UV housing before it is returned to the aquarium. While in the housing, the water is exposed to the UV light which kills most bacteria and protozoa. You should trouble-shoot UV and strip lights the same.

Lighting Tips
Place strip lights toward the front of the tank for better illumination of the fish. Periodically check that water or salt has not seeped into the plastic reflector hood housing and caused corrosion. Be careful when handling fluorescent strip and UV light bulbs since they contain toxic gasses.

UV light bulbs can lose effective strength long before burning out. Therefore, even if the bulb is lit, it may have no sterilizing effect. The effective life of the bulb is dependent on the amount of time it is used. Refer to the owners manual for your specific bulb's effective strength duration. Don't forget that UV lights work the same as fluorescent lights when power is lost and then returns, you will need to turn the UV light back on again. You should not look directly into a lit UV bulb. You should also periodically replace the rubber seals that protect the electrical connections to the UV bulb.

Light Problems
Always remember to disconnect all electrical devices from the power source before you begin any repair. The only components that can fail in aquarium lighting are the bulb, starter and ballast (a ballast is a type of transformer that regulates the current to the starter and bulb). Trouble-shoot strip and UV lights in the following manner.

Light Comes on Dim or Slowly - A faulty starter usually causes this problem and should be replaced. If it is not the starter, replace the ballast (if you have an extra bulb, try that first just to be sure before you buy a ballast).

Light Doesn't Come On - Trouble-shoot the light in the following order; check electrical connections including the switch and circuit breaker (some UV and strip lights have internal circuit breakers), make sure the bulb is properly seated. If no trouble is found replace the bulb. If that is not the problem replace the starter. The last option is to replace the ballast.

Rubber Seal on UV Bulb Leaks - Replace all seals. Do not operate the light with a leaking seal!

Inlet/Outlet Connection Leaks - See Box, Canister or Tubing Leaks under **WATER FILTERS**.

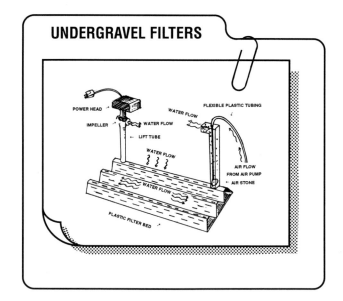

UNDERGRAVEL FILTERS

Filters placed beneath the aquarium gravel are used in some aquariums as a debris filter and biological breeding bed for beneficial bacteria (see Biological Filter Cycle in **WATER CHEMISTRY**). The undergravel filter is a raised plastic bed that covers the bottom of the aquarium and has about two inches of the desired substrate (filter medium) placed on top. The substrate usually consists of natural shells and stones such as crushed oyster shells, dolomite, calcite, coral, limestone, or silica sand. Lift tubes placed at the opposite ends of the filter use either forced air or water pumps (called power heads) to pull water from the tank, through the substrate, and up and out the lift tubes at the water's surface.

Power Heads
Power heads are used in place of airstones in the lift tubes in order to dramatically increase the flow rate of the water. The power heads house a motor that drives an impeller and pulls the water up the lift tube and out near the surface.

Undergravel Filter Tips
To avoid cloudy water, thoroughly wash the gravel under running water before you place it in the tank. Periodically rake the gravel and remove the debris with a siphon. Never use a plastic filter bed that is broken (see Broken or Clogged Filter Section below).

Undergravel Filter Problems
Always remember to disconnect all electrical devices from the power source before you begin any repair.

Power Head Won't Pump Water - Occasionally a stone from the gravel bottom will be sucked up the lift tube, into the power head and jam the impeller. Take off the appropriate power head cover to gain access to the impeller and remove the stone. If a jammed impeller is not the problem, check all electrical connections. If no problem is found, the motor is suspect.

Air Flow to Lift Tubes has Decreased - See Air Flow has Decreased under **AIR PUMPS**.

Broken or Clogged Filter Section - The plastic filter bed has several long, raised, tunnel-like sections that serve as piping for the water to reach to the lift tubes. If a section is broken or the holes in the plastic bed have increased in size because of damage, gravel can be sucked through the hole. The gravel will then either block that portion of the filter making it ineffective, or be sucked up the lift tubes and jam the power head impellers. The broken section can be repaired with silicone sealant. Do not use glues since they can be toxic to the fish.

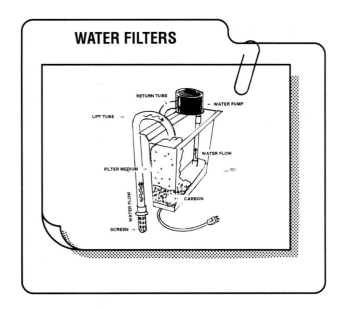

Water filters are used to rid the tank of the waste materials of fish, plants and uneaten food. The two most common powered water filters for aquariums are plastic box filters that hang on the back of the tank or the external canister filters, usually placed below the tank, which can move large volumes of water. Both types incorporate the same filtration design principal.

Plastic lift tubes placed in the tank water are connected to the inlet of the canister filters or empty into the plastic holding tank of the box filter. A motor drives an impeller which pumps the water from the aquarium, through a filter medium, and back into the aquarium using return tubes. While in the filter, the water is passed through either synthetic floss, rock, charcoal or some other filter medium where the undesired waste material is collected and then periodically discarded by the aquarist.

Water Filter Tips
Be aware that the filter medium contains harmful bacteria caused by decaying waste from fish and plants. If this material is left stagnant for any significant period of time, the bacteria causes a buildup of concentrated toxic nitrites which, if pumped into the tank, could be lethal. Therefore, if the power is lost to the aquarium or you shut off the water pump for more than two hours, discard the filter medium, and the water from the box or canister and prime the filter before turning the pump back on.

Make sure the screens on the lift tubes are not missing or broken or the pump may suck a small fish into the filter's plastic tank. It's easier and less messy to use a priming stick with a plug on its end rather than the palm of your hand to prime the filter pumps. Periodically check all tubing and connections for leaks.

Water Filter Problems

Always remember to disconnect all electrical devices from the power source before you begin any repair.

Box, Canister or Tubing Leaks - Rubber seals will corrode, especially when used with salt water. Check all seals and replace if necessary. If any tubing or connections leak, use silicone sealant for repair. The pump will have to be turned off and the tubing allowed to dry before applying the sealant. It may take a few days for the silicone to cure so be aware of the bacteria build up during this period as described in the tips above. Increase aeration during this time period. If the leaks continue, replace the defective plastic tubing, joints or connections.

Pump Doesn't Move Water - If the motor hums but doesn't pump water, the pump may have sucked a small stone from the bottom gravel and it has jammed the impeller. Removing the stone will fix the problem. If the motor doesn't hum, check all electrical connections including switches and circuit breakers (some pumps have an internal breaker). If no trouble is found, the motor has probably failed.

Decreased Water Flow - When the water flow seems to have decreased, check the flow control setting on the pump (if it has one). Next, check for clogged or very dirty filter medium. Also check for obstructions to lift tubes, inlets, outlets, or crimped hoses, poor connections and leaks. If no trouble is found, the motor may be getting weak and may have to be replaced.

LAST RESORT

Occasionally, you may find that you are unable to make a diagnosis using the flow charts. Your fish may be sick or acting strange. You know something is wrong but are unsure what to do. In this case, check once again for an environmental problem. Use the Poisoning, Water Problem, and Equipment Problem flow charts to ensure that an environmental problem does not exist. Pay special attention to equipment, such as power heads, air pumps and water pumps that may have become faulty.

Perform a 25% water change and increase aeration. This therapy never hurts and if the problem is water quality, the fish should perk up in a few hours.

If the fish is just sluggish with no other symptoms, it may be constipated (see **CONSTIPATION**). If the fish has been fed a constant diet of flake foods, alter the food every other day for a week with frozen green peas (let them thaw for a few minutes before placing in the tank) or Tetra vegetable flake food. Whatever the fish's diet, alter it for a week and see if the condition improves.

If the problem remains or becomes worse, get additional help by doing an information search. Call several trusted aquarium dealers, experienced fish hobbyists or public aquariums and explain the problem. Search for more detailed books on fish diseases, their symptoms and treatment. If, after you have exhausted your information search and still have found no solution, you have no choice but to make assumptions and treat the fish for the general diseases.

Remember too, fish sometimes die with no visible symptoms and for no apparent reason. Many times the cause cannot be determined without a postmortem by a trained fish disease pathologist. If you have tried all the steps described below and your fish dies, be assured you did your best. Learn from the experience and note any mistakes you may have made.

Symptoms: You are unable to make a diagnosis. There are no visible symptoms, but the fish is not behaving normally and may have stopped eating. The fish's condition has continued for a few days and may be getting worse. Something is definitely wrong and you have concluded that the fish needs medication.

Treatment: You should treat the fish for the most common bacterial and parasitic diseases by following the steps described below. Throughout the treatment periods, look for any new primary or secondary symptoms. If the fish develops a distinctive symptom, use the flow charts to diagnose the problem and switch to that recommended treatment.

Step 1 - Gill/Skin Fluke Treatment:
In some instances, a minor case of gill or skin flukes can cause fish to act strange but have no other visible symptoms. Therefore, a quick diagnostic therapy for saltwater fish would be to give it a formalin bath. If gill flukes are the problem, the symptoms will disappear within 48 hours after the bath. Follow the instructions for Formalin Bath in **GILL & SKIN FLUKES**.

If the problem remains, or if the problem is with a freshwater fish, treatment should be made in a hospital tank as follows (if you must add drugs to the main tank, see **MAIN TANK MEDICATION**).

> a) Make a 30% water change to the main tank, increase aeration and let the water cycle through all the aquarium filters for two hours, then proceed to step b.

> b) Set up the hospital tank (see **HOSPITAL TANK**) and siphon water from the main tank into the hospital tank. Provide strong aeration to the hospital tank.

c) Place the fish in the hospital tank.

d) If the fish is a freshwater fish, add one teaspoon of sea salt solution per gallon.

Medication:

The assumption you now have to make is that the fish is diseased. The most common fish diseases are either bacterial or parasitic in origin. Each disease requires a different treatment therapy including different medication. Therefore, you should probably treat the fish for a bacterial infection first as described below. If the problem is not eliminated, treat for parasites as described later.

Step 2 - Bacterial Treatment:

Use the following procedures to treat the fish against a possible bacterial infection.

a) Treat the fish with one of the broad spectrum antibiotics listed in **BACTERIAL INFECTION**. Treat the fish for an additional three days beyond the recommended time to make sure all the bacteria is killed.

b) Feed the fish only Tetra Medicated Flake food (antibacterial/antifungal) for a period of two weeks. Continue to feed this even if the fish has been cured and placed back in the main tank.

Observe the fish closely for a few days for signs of improvement. If the fish returns to normal, the treatment has probably been sufficient. If the fish does not respond to this therapy, go to Step 3.

Step 3 - Invisible Ick:

There is a form of Ick, called Invisible Ick, that cannot be seen on a fish's body. Although more rare than Ick, a fish infected with this parasite may have similar secondary symptoms such as sluggishness and it may have stopped eating. Treatment for this disease is the same as for Ick.

a) Make an 80% water change in the hospital tank by siphoning water again from the main tank.

b) Switch from Tetra's antibacterial/antifungal medicated flake food to the antiparasitic food for a two week period. If the fish is a freshwater fish, also continue the salt treatment described in Step 1 (d) above.

c) Medicate the fish with the same drugs used for Ick (see **ICK**). If the fish does not respond to this therapy, go to Step 4.

Step 4 - Other Parasites:

The fish could also have other parasites that are either internal or external but are not visible. A good therapy for unknown parasites would be the same as for the treatment against camallanus worms.

a) Make another 80% water change to the hospital tank by siphoning water again from the main tank.

b) Continue feeding the antiparasitic Tetra Medicated Flake food for the remainder of the treatment period. If the fish is a freshwater fish, continue the salt treatment described in Step 1 (d) above.

c) Treat the fish according to **CAMALLANUS WORMS**.

Appendix

Conversion Tables
Formulas
Graphs
Charts
Index

Aquarium Maintenance Guidelines

Activity	Daily	Weekly	Monthly
Visual check of fish for headcount, disease, swimming and breathing rates	✓		
Check color, smell and temperature of water		✓	
Visual check of equipment, air and water flow		✓	
Scrape algae growth on glass			✓
Check and prune plants			✓
Rake and siphon debris from gravel bottom			✓
Make a 25% water change (every 2 to 4 weeks)			✓
Change air and water filters			✓
Test water chemistry			✓

Length

Convert To...

	mm	cm	meter	inch	feet	yard
mm	-	.1	.001	.039	.0033	.0011
cm	10	-	.01	.394	.033	.011
meter	1000	100	-	39.4	3.28	1.09
inch	25.4	2.54	.025	-	.083	.027
feet	305	30.5	.31	12	-	.333
yard	915	91.4	.91	36	3	-

Convert From...

Multipliers

Instructions: 1. Choose from the left column what measurement to convert from. 2. Choose from the top row what measurement to convert to. 3. Use the multiplier at the intersection of the selected row and column and multiply by the original measurement.

Weight

Convert To...

	mg	gram	kg	ounce	pound
mg	-	.001	.000001	.00004	.000002
gram	1000	-	.001	.035	.0022
kg	1000000	1000	-	35.3	2.2
ounce	28,300	28.35	.028	-	.0625
pound	453,600	454	.454	16	-

Convert From...

Multipliers

Instructions: 1. Choose from the left column what measurement to convert from. 2. Choose from the top row what measurement to convert to. 3. Use the multiplier at the intersection of the selected row and column and multiply by the original measurement.

Volume

Convert To...

Convert From...	ml	liter	tsp	tbsp	fl oz	cup	pint	quart	US gal
ml	-	.001	.2	.067	.034	.0042	.0021	.001	.0003
liter	1000	-	200	67	34	4.22	2.11	1.06	.264
tsp	5	.005	-	.33	.167	.021	.01	.0053	.0013
tbsp	15	.015	3	-	.5	.0625	.032	.0159	.004
fl oz	30	.03	6	2	-	.125	.064	.032	.008
cup	237	.237	48	16	8	-	.5	.25	.063
pint	473	.473	96	32	16	2	-	.5	.125
quart	946	.946	192	64	32	4	2	-	.25
US gal	3784	3.79	768	256	128	16	8	4	-

Multipliers

Instructions: 1. Choose from the left column what measurement to convert from. 2. Choose from the top row what measurement to convert to. 3. Use the multiplier at the intersection of the selected row and column and multiply by the original measurement.

US/UK Conversions

Convert To...

Convert From...	US gal	UK gal	liter
US gal	-	.83	3.785
UK gal	1.25	-	4.55
liter	.26	.22	

Multipliers

PPM Conversions

Convert To...

Convert From...	mg/liter	gm/liter	ppm
mg/liter	-	.001	1
gm/liter	1000	-	1000
ppm	1	.001	-

Multipliers

Note: 1 mg/liter is equal to 1 ppm. Therefore, a 1% ppm solution is 10,000 parts per 1,000,000 or 10 grams per liter (38 grams per US gallon).

Seawater Composition

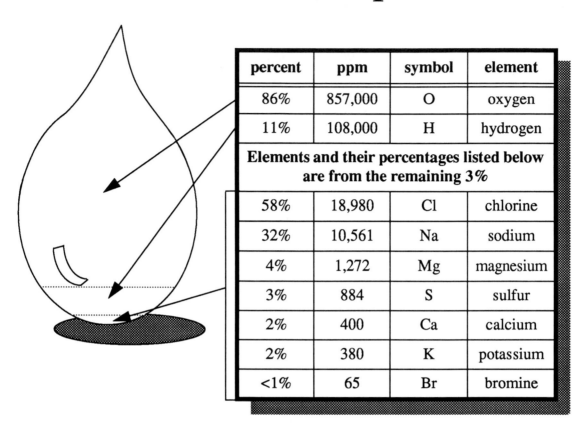

percent	ppm	symbol	element
86%	857,000	O	oxygen
11%	108,000	H	hydrogen
Elements and their percentages listed below are from the remaining 3%			
58%	18,980	Cl	chlorine
32%	10,561	Na	sodium
4%	1,272	Mg	magnesium
3%	884	S	sulfur
2%	400	Ca	calcium
2%	380	K	potassium
<1%	65	Br	bromine

1 gallon

Weight of Water

1 US gallon of water weighs 8.33 pounds or 3.78 kilograms. One liter of water weighs 1 kilogram or 2.2 pounds.

Temperature

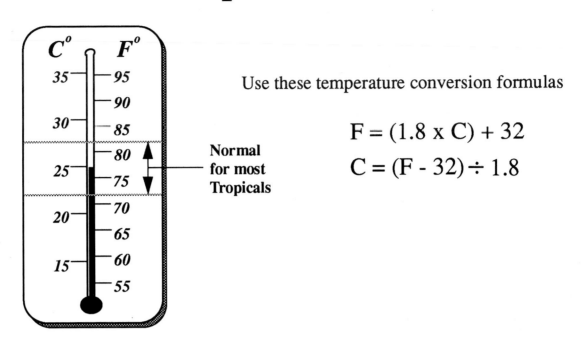

Use these temperature conversion formulas

$$F = (1.8 \times C) + 32$$
$$C = (F - 32) \div 1.8$$

Normal for most Tropicals

pH Scale

Freshwater Range (6.5 - 7.5)   Saltwater Range (8.1 - 8.5)

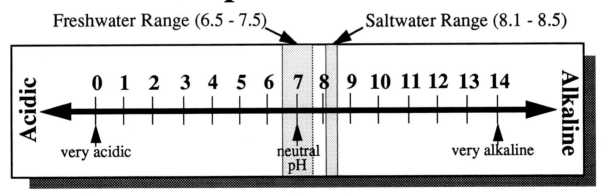

The pH (pondus Hydrogenni or Hydrogen power) scale determines the acidity or alkalinity of water by measuring the concentration of hydrogen ions. The more ion concentration, the more acid the water and lower the pH. The less ion concentration the more alkaline the water and higher the pH.

A log scale is used to measure pH. Therefore, since 7 is neutral, an 8 reading indicates 10 times <u>less</u> hydrogen ion concentration, and a 6 reading would mean 10 times <u>more</u> hydrogen ion concentration.

For most freshwater tropical fish, the desired pH range is 6.5 - 7.5 and the marine range is 8.1 - 8.5. Your aquarium's pH level can be adjusted using buffers of sodium phosphates and bicarbonates. Refer also to pH under **WATER CHEMISTRY**.

Fish Morphology and Anatomy

Fish Morphology

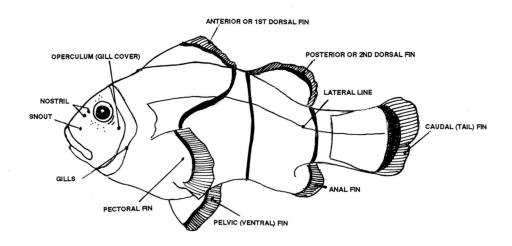

Fish Anatomy

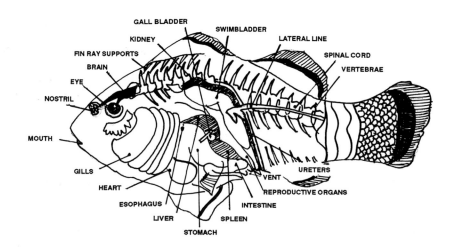

Biological Filter Cycle

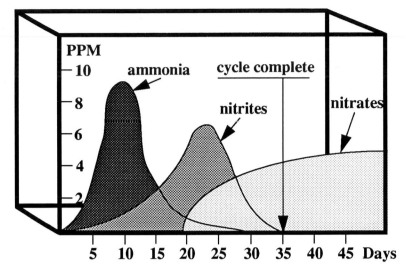

The biological filter cycle is the process that transforms new gravel filter beds into an established biological filter. During this period, fish waste decays forming bacteria and ammonia in the filter bed. As the bacteria level rises, it transforms the ammonia into nitrites. At this stage, the toxicity levels peak and are the most lethal to fish. The bacteria eventually transforms the nitrites into less toxic nitrates. When the ammonia and nitrite levels reach near zero, the cycle is complete and more delicate fish can be added at that time.

The above example is a common model of a biological filter cycle. The actual toxicity levels and number of days required for completion of the cycle depends on tank size, number of fish, water changes and the amount of oxygen in the water. For more information, see Biological Filter Cycle in **Poisoning**.

^{o}*DH - Hardness Scale*

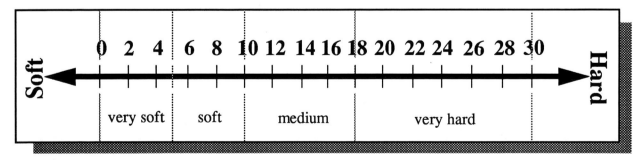

The degree of water hardness is measured on the German DH scale. Hardness is determined by the level of impurities in the water such as dissolved salt, calcium and magnesium. Water hardness can be adjusted by filtration, boiling or adding chemicals such as sodium carbonate. Although water hardness is not as much of a concern for the aquarist as is pH, it can be a factor for specialty fish keeping and breeding. Refer also to Water Hardness in **WATER CHEMISTRY**.

BIBLIOGRAPHY

Bodie, Scott *Confessions of a Fish Doctor.*
New York: Workman Publishing Co., 1977.

Geisler, Rolf *Aquarium Fish Diseases.*
Neptune City, NJ: TFH Publications, 1963.

Hodgson, Edward S. and Robert F. Mathewson *Sensory Biology of Sharks, Skates and Rays.*
Arlington: Office of Naval Research, Department of the Navy, 1978.

Kingsford, Edward *Treatment of Exotic Marine Fish Diseases.*
New York: Arco Publishing Co., 1975.

Klocek, Roger *Observations on Coral and Anemone Degenerative Diseases.*
AAZPA Annual Conference Proceedings, pp. 773-775, 1986.

Lanier, Robert J. and Ida M. Mellen *1001 Questions Answered About Your Aquarium.*
New York: Dodd, Mead & Co., 1961.

Scheurmann, Ines *The New Aquarium Handbook.*
New York: Barron's, 1985.

Schubert, Gottfried *Cure and Recognize Aquarium Fish Disease.*
Neptune City, NJ: TFH Publications, 1974.

Snieszko, Stanislas F. and Herbert R. Axelrod *Diseases of Fishes* Books 2A & 2B.
Neptune City, NJ: TFH Publications, 1971.

Straughan, Robert P.L. *Keeping Sea Horses.*
Neptune City, NJ: TFH Publications, 1961.

Van Duijn, C. *Diseases of Fishes.*
Springfield, IL: Charles C. Thomas, 1973.

Index

Fish Diseases

Medications

Equipment Problems

Organize Your Aquarium Hobby!

The full potential of this book is met when it is used with the book *The Complete Aquarium Logbook*, available at your aquarium dealer from **Tetra Press**. Use the Problem Solving book to diagnose fish and aquatic animal diseases, or to trouble-shoot water and equipment problems. Then use the Logbook to record all problems discovered, therapy given or repairs made.